Your Life Can Be Creative Adventure!

There is no end to the spiritual frontier. You can go out into life purposefully, usefully and with pride in yourself.

Here, in this indispensable guide for living in the modern world today—loaded with stories, packed with advice, complete with fifteen valuable mental exercises utilizing self-image psychology—Dr. Maltz shows you how.

Maxwell Maltz, M.D., F.I.C.S., received his baccalaureate in science from Columbia University and his doctorate in medicine at Columbia's College of Physicians and Surgeons. One of the world's most renowned plastic surgeons, he practiced in England, France, Germany, Italy and Latin America. He lectured before the University of Amsterdam, the University of Paris and the University of Rome. He was Professor of Plastic Surgery at the University of Nicaragua and the University of El Salvador. He was the author of eleven books, among them *Adventures in Staying Young*, and the best sellers *Doctor Pygmalion* and *Psycho-Cybernetics*.

Most Pocket Books are available at special quantity discounts for bulk
purchases for sales promotions, premiums or fund raising. Special
books or book excerpts can also be created to fit specific needs.

For details write or telephone the office of the Vice President of Special
Markets, Pocket Books, 1230 Avenue of the Americas, New York, New
York 10020. (212) 245-6400, ext. 1760.

Maxwell Maltz, M.D., F.I.C.S.

CREATIVE
LIVING
FOR
TODAY

PUBLISHED BY POCKET BOOKS NEW YORK

POCKET BOOKS, a Simon & Schuster division of
GULF & WESTERN CORPORATION
1230 Avenue of the Americas, New York, N Y 10020

Copyright © 1967 by Dr Maxwell Maltz

Published by arrangement with Trident Press a Simon & Schuster
division of Gulf & Western Corporation
Library of Congress Catalog Card Number 67-26453

ISBN 0-671-46767-0

First Pocket Books printing April, 1970

20 19 18 17 16

POCKET and colophon are registered trademarks
of Simon & Schuster

Printed in the U S.A.

Preface

PEOPLE LIVE longer and longer lives these days; they benefit from government concern with their problems and from our rising standard of living. Yet they find living difficult.

I am writing this book because the need is so great, because people's years are so wasted.

Our whole concept of living has been false; there is a drastic need to change our thinking.

We must do something about the uselessness which so many people feel; we must do something to give them back their feeling of human worth; we must help them to reassert their belief in their own self-respect.

In the last ten or twenty years we have seen the beginnings of a determined drive to win for Negroes their rights of equal opportunity and human self-respect; the same should be done for people in general, who are victims not of prejudice, but of inertia.

The individual citizen must gear himself to meet the challenges of creative living. He must will a positive change in his life pattern, in his attitude toward himself and in his image of himself as he moves constructively into the flow of life around him.

One purpose of this book is to show people that they need not retreat from life into a negative pattern of living, that they can live creatively in this century of pessimism.

People must learn that when they set purposeful goals and make it a daily habit to attain them, their lives will have meaning. They must understand that life is more than a succession of twenty-four-hour vacuums. All people must understand that creative living starts *now*.

The chief enemy of creative living is the passive patterns into which people fall; telling themselves that they are meaningless specks in a huge world, they tend to pamper themselves on a diet of entertainment and become "watchers" in a world that passes them by.

It is a basic idea of mine that while you are living, you *live*. Your days are full of goals. You work to strengthen your internal resources, the success instincts within all of you, so that you go out toward the world with the best that is in you. You build a more satisfying mental image of yourself. You see that it is the concept of your own worth as a person that activates and reactivates the functioning of your success mechanism, your built-in capacity to achieve fulfillment, or plunges you backward into a series of failures. Thus you work to pump health and more health into your self-image, steering your mind toward productive goals, which is my concept of psycho-cybernetics.

Too much negative thinking is eating into people's minds these days. Too many people waste their lives feeling depressed, asking what is life for.

I feel that my book will give you this hope: that life can be an adventure, that there are still new horizons, that there is no end to the spiritual frontier.

Your years need not be lived in an emotional dungeon; you can go out into life purposefuly, usefully, and with pride in yourself.

It is only realistic to say that, in this "age of anxiety," your years can be happy ones.

MAXWELL MALTZ, M.D.

Contents

CREATIVE
LIVING
FOR
TODAY

• 1 •

The Search for Your
Creative Powers

LIFE SHOULD BE a fruitful, growing adventure for all of us. As creatures of the natural world, transcending animal limitations with our unique mental equipment, we have been endowed with potent tools for forging happiness.

Green trees and cool blue waters around us give pleasure to our senses and supply us with fruit and fish to eat, while high in the sky the sun pours its warmth down upon us. Below us the fertile soil promises us rich vegetables to nourish our organs.

The horse and the dog are our friends; the cow and the chicken give us milk and eggs and meat. From love and natural desire come babies, who grow into children and later assume the responsibilities of adults in our community. Inside us flows our blood, renewing our tissues; the most efficient machine ever created works inside our bodies.

More than all this, our mind is ours and, with it, we can create. We have created mechanistic marvels: automobiles, skyscrapers, airplanes, refrigerators, air conditioners, television, satellites in outer space. With it, we can create contentment, contentment in a joyful world in which we can harness machines to eliminate most of the dangers and hardships.

Not only is it our potential to build meaningful lives, it is also our obligation to ourselves.

And yet the quest for happiness is, to so many people, a grotesque traffic jam. The motor keeps running, but the car can't move.

Too many people have renounced happiness; too many feel that living has lost its kick for them; too many find no purpose in their days.

Why is this? Why do people give up on life? Why do they give up on themselves?

"The pace is too fast," some say. They point to cars which roar sixty-five miles an hour on our highways, to jets which whiz six hundred miles an hour in the skies. They talk about the hustle-bustle of city life, the speed with which people move around on working days. They criticize the changes in our ideas: about sex, about art, about dress. Who can keep up with these revolutions in thought?

"Individuality is dead," others say. "Large corporations dominate business; the small businessman is losing out; automation is hurting people. People are becoming data, to be filed into the giant machine hopper en route to their dehumanization."

"Mankind is doomed," others proclaim. "Each year more and more nations possess nuclear weapons. Sooner or later there will be a nuclear holocaust. Even if we avoid this, radioactive fallout will kill us slowly."

All right, there is some truth to the criticisms of today's world, I will not deny that. No thinking person will claim that we live in a perfect world, or that we live in a world without tremendous dangers.

But people have always lived with imperfection and with danger. Down through history we find people coping with problems; some lived richly, some were afraid to live.

And so it is today. There are people who live, and people who use rationalizations to keep them from living fully.

Criticisms of the modern world serve only as stumbling blocks if they lead people to turn away from life. These criticisms are invalid if this, rather than constructive appraisal, is their purpose.

There is no excuse for negative thinking which wastes human life. When a person drowns himself in such a pattern of thinking, he is committing an unspeakable crime against himself.

Yet in our complex civilization people too often live with boredom or anxiety rather than adventure.

As I begin to write this book on creative living, I look forward to each chapter—each page—with enthusiasm. Because I want to communicate to you my ideas on the meaning of life. Because I yearn to tell you about the good life which you can make reality.

I have written many books; never was there one I wanted more to write.

I feel that I have a certain perspective. Being over sixty-five, I have experienced for a long time the problems of a human being who wants to make the most of his life. I have been there, with my eyes open, and I feel that what my eyes have seen your eyes may share.

I want to share my truth with you: *that zestful, optimistic living can be a reality for people today.*

So many people do not see this truth; rationalizations obscure it and defeatism crushes it. Yet it is as real as the table at which you eat; it is as real as the fact that you are male or female.

Contrary to what many think, truth can be pleasant.

Operating on Your Mind

I have been a plastic surgeon for about forty years. I have improved the physical images of hundreds, thousands, of people. This is constructive, satisfying work.

I have strengthened chins, remodeled noses, removed disfiguring scars. I have eliminated excess tissue and wrinkles from the skin.

That many people have come to me is testimony to their concern with their physical image. And why not? Why shouldn't any person care about the way he looks? A mature person should care.

As a plastic surgeon, I have helped many people to feel better about themselves. Still, there is more to life than a good physical image. There is another force which can sustain you amid the demands of living. *It is a force that can remove scars from the mind.* It is a force that can bring you a sense of security, even when events in your world go wrong.

It is your self-image.

In *Hamlet,* Shakespeare wrote, "To take arms against a sea of troubles."

To live creatively, you must "take arms." You must arm

yourself with powerful weapons which will not fire blanks when you need their support.

There is this potency in a strong self-image—abstract as it may sound, there is enormous potency in it—and I will tell you about it in the pages of this book.

Don't Let Worries Get You Down!

It is deplorable how negative thinking can take hold of you, dragging you down into despair.

Gloom and worry dominate the thinking of so many people today.

The college student who spends half his time worrying about radioactive fallout knows nothing of real living. Sure he can try to realistically improve the situation—he can write his congressman or organize a group to discuss the problem—but when he buries his being in worry, this is only self-destruction.

The young mother whose thoughts are full of anxiety about her children is also wasting her days. Not that she shouldn't teach them about life's dangers, not that she shouldn't try to protect them from catastrophe, but, after that, why the self-torture? It won't help.

The middle-aged businessman who is obsessed with money —is not something in him dead? Of course, money is important. But, what good will obsessive fears do? Positive, creative planning—that's something else.

All these worries—and more—you can justify if you wish. You can tell yourself you are only being realistic, but you're really not.

Otherwise, there would be no Helen Kellers, no Franklin Roosevelts, to overcome their physical handicaps and go on to lives of greatness. There would be no Winston Churchills to rise up in times of crisis and stand like rocks in the face of tyranny.

No, when you substitute worry for living, you must take the responsibility for it.

Because it's really up to you. *You* can make your days thrilling, or *you* can make them miserable.

Still, if you've wasted some of your life moping, don't

blame yourself for it. You're not perfect, no one is, and self-blame will not help you. Just read what I have to say and see if my ideas won't help you to live more meaningfully.

The Source of Your Strength

To bring health into your life, you need a healthy self-image. You need to see yourself as a worthwhile human being; you must give acceptance to yourself.

In *Psycho-Cybernetics* and in *The Magic Power of Self-Image Psychology* I described in detail how I arrived at my concept of the self-image.

As a plastic surgeon, time and again I improved people's physical features. Perhaps I would improve the construction of a person's nose or sharpen the lines of his chin. With the improvement, his reaction was usually one of pleasure when he looked in the mirror and saw his new image.

"There I am," he would seem to feel, "I look better than ever before. It will be a better world for me."

These cases were satisfying. My patient would feel happy with his improved image and I would feel that my work was meaningful.

Other people, however, reacted in a way which puzzled me, until I came to understand how they felt. They would look in the mirror and freeze into indifference; truly, though their appearance was improved, they could not enjoy the change.

I came to understand the underlying meaning of their reactions when I talked to a number of these people. Because of unfortunate factors in their lives, invariably stemming from childhood or adolescence, they felt inferior and faced the world with defeatist, dejected, or hostile attitudes.

The change in their physical image meant nothing to them, so weak was their concept of themselves as people—so weak was their self-image.

The lesson I learned from these experiences in understanding, deeply felt because I wanted to serve these people, will always be with me. It did not injure my confidence in the value of plastic surgery as a tool for helping people. There is no question that one should look as well as one can. But I learned, in addition, that the image one has of himself, the way he sees himself deep down, is fundamental in his adjustment to himself and to the world he lives in.

Sharpening Your Image of Yourself

My aim in writing this book is to help you strengthen this self-image so that you will tackle your life situations healthfully, without allowing prejudice against yourself to eat its way into your mind.

This is no easy task, and I'm not saying that it is. Deeply ingrained negative attitudes permeate our culture, and every day people you know may try to submerge you in them. You must not allow yourself to be railroaded into adopting stereotyped, humiliating attitudes toward yourself.

In your teens and twenties you may hear that you are unlucky. Voices of gloom may tell you that automation will not allow you to be creative in work, that it is your bad fortune to be young in an age in which the individual is nothing. You may go toward life with one attitude—despair.

In your middle years you may hear that the world is too complex, that this age places demands on the individual's shoulders which are too heavy. So you may reach out toward others with one attitude—negation.

In your later years you may feel that you are no longer useful. You may feel your life is over, while many years remain. So you, too, will feel despair.

True, these are not easy years for people; no years ever have been. But, still, there are wonders in life to explore; there are good moments to live. We must bury our negative thinking and feel the exciting promise of each day.

There is much hope for people today; there is hope for people who understand how to work with themselves for their own betterment.

You must, to live creatively, redouble your efforts to support yourself, to give yourself credit for your accomplishments, your positive feelings, your positive actions, your life-building qualities. You must also redouble your efforts to accept your shortcomings and to look humanely upon your blunders. Moreover, you must specifically examine yourself as you are, realistically, without falling prey to negative ideas which would shortchange your estimate of yourself.

If your self-image was never strong, you must work long and hard to strengthen it. If it was once strong but has deteriorated, you must eliminate self-destructive ideas from your mind and build it again—a logical continuation of what it used to be.

You will encounter roadblocks from many sources, but you can overcome them if you adopt positive attitudes toward yourself, and if you see yourself as someone you like, as someone with whom you'd like to be friends.

You must understand, first, the incredible power of your mind —for good or evil. It is not easy to comprehend that in a world of skyscrapers and superhighways, of atomic energy and astronauts speeding through outer space, it is the simple concepts and images in your mind that can make you happy or miserable.

But this is so. *Your thoughts, your concepts, your images,* these are your most precious assets. You can buy a Cadillac *and* a mink coat *and* an expensive house—and be unhappy. You can see yourself as a friend would—and be content. You can circle the globe a hundred times and make a million dollars, too—and be miserable. You can strengthen your image of yourself—and be content.

Real Meaning in Your Life

Life is something different for each person. Sad to say, some people hide, afraid to come out into the daylight. Others may take refuge in safe, dull activities which will protect them from both punishment and real human experience. There are many mechanisms with which people live out their days, enduring the boredom, tensing themselves to absorb the pain.

But life should be an adventure for you—today.

Life should be exciting for you—today.

Life should be purposeful for you—today.

This is what we will explore in the pages of this book: the road toward the adventurous, exciting, purposeful life. I will locate for you the keys to dynamic hours, creative days, meaningful years.

You must understand that you can help yourself; I will show you how. I will tell you about people like yourself—no matter how wealthy or how successful, how secure or how mature, they *are* like yourself—and how they harnessed their powers for constructive living. We will work together on fifteen concrete exercises which will strengthen your resolution.

You must understand that, though we seem to hear mostly the negative, there are two sides to the coin. Even within the many confines of civilzation, the human being may still be free and joyous.

Ralph Waldo Emerson once wrote that "The life of man is the true romance, which, when it is valiantly conducted, will yield the imagination a higher joy than any fiction."

This was written in the nineteenth century, but it is still accurate—if one's life is "valiantly conducted."

One final thought before I launch into the body of my book: *Preparation for rich living cannot start too soon.* Now, now is the time.

Now is the time to reappraise yourself—who you are, where you are going. *Now* is the time to see what you can do to improve your life.

It is my hope that all readers will find refreshment and perhaps some common sense, too, in these pages.

• 2 •

Security in an
Uncertain World

"UNCERTAINTY" IS a key word in our lives. We must live with uncertainty and steer our ship through life's perilous paths—or retreat from life into a womb, an illusion, or boredom.

Since there are few guarantees to reassure us, we must learn to master these dangers to the best of our ability, and still live contentedly.

After the "traumatic" process of our birth, we live the uncertain, minute-by-minute moments of infants in which a tolerant smile is followed by an indignant roar of rage and a howl of laughter—all within the space of thirty seconds.

Then come the uncertainties of childhood, in which we depend on our parents, whose destinies fluctuate according to complex economic, emotional, and sociological factors which we cannot yet understand.

The period of adolescence that follows is even more uncertain. Are we children or adults—or what are we? How should we behave toward adults? What is this thing called sex; is it good or bad and whose opinion do you ask and what do you do about it? Why do my parents still treat me like a child. I'm grown-up—or am I?

Adulthood brings with it new problems, new uncertainties. The choice of vocations, the decisions to be made about marriage and marriage partner and children and sexual activities, about business commitments and political views and insurance protection and community participation or noninvolvement, gambling or non-gambling strategies—I could write pages and pages on the conflicts a responsible adult must face and the uncertainties surrounding his decisions and the outcomes of his considered choices.

The retirement years, too, bring problems: enforced idleness and, at its sharpest, fear of death.

Throughout their lives most people worry about tragedy striking—the breadwinner losing his job, a fire that wipes out one's home, an automobile accident in which a loved one is crippled—and these are real possibilities that one must learn to live with without burying his head in the sand.

What is the answer to these dilemmas of life?

It is simple, really. *More life, reaffirmation of life, while there is life*—life, with the help of a healthy self-image that will give you the sense of certainty you need.

Someday we will all die, that is God's law of life and there is nothing we can do about it. But, while we lived, did we *live?*

Did we live—or did we just occupy space while we went through the motions of living? Did we enjoy every year, every month, every week, every day—or did we manage to passively endure the dull moments? Did we *see* the green trees, *smell* the beautiful flowers, *share* with our friends, *taste* our lamb chops, *love* our work—or were we so obsessed with worry that life could not enter into our troubled minds?

As babies, we are born with a smile coming through the first howl of pain. While we live, we must live constructively so that time and again a smile might break through the pain.

Now, what about friendships—one of the chief ingredients of a rich life?

Man's Best Friend

There is a saying to the effect that "the dog is man's best friend," but I do not automatically fall in with silly sayings like this. I am fond of dogs but, if my observations are correct, a dog will be far from your best friend if you do not take care of him in the style to which he is accustomed.

Man's best friend—any man's best friend—is his self-image. If he sees himself as a good guy, he's on the road to contentment; if he doesn't, he will cause his own downfall.

John or Tom or Alice or Eleanor may be your friend—and may be a valued friend—but your best friend is your self-image. Another person may like you, may even go out of his way to help you in a crisis, but he cannot live for you. He cannot make your decisions, cannot participate completely in your joys and heartbreaks; more, he cannot give you the capacity for success or failure, for self-acceptance or self-rejection.

Your self-image can give you this capacity. It can give you a sense of certainty as you live. If you see yourself as agreeable, if your picture of yourself is satisfying, you live with a marvelous form of certainty: the conviction that when uncontrollable factors go against you and events temporarily oppose your desires, you will support yourself.

There will always be moments of adversity hitting you from the external world, as well as self-doubts plaguing you from within. The real test of your friendship for yourself is whether you rally to your own aid when you need the consoling sustenance of your best friend—you.

When you are sure of this internal cushion in crisis, then you know how to be certain in this uncertain world.

Do Not Commit Spiritual Suicide!

It is easy to rationalize.

You can say to yourself, "But the uncertainty *is* real; how *can* I relax?" You may protest that my point of view is not realistic.

But I assure you that it is.

And I assure you that I, too, know of life's dangers.

Let me tell you a story. Suppose you manufacture a picture in your mind of this scene: A man of fifty, stocky build, walrus mustache, walks on the sidewalk. He is hurrying; there is an eager look on his face, as if he is anticipating some pleasure. He is heading for the entrance to the subway at the end of the block. As he nears it, a truck, out of control, comes hurtling onto the sidewalk and crashes into him, knocking him on his back. People rush to his aid, but it is too late. He is dead.

Now switch scenes in your mind to the lobby of a New York hospital. A young man in white, intern's uniform, paces back and forth; people in the lobby look at him curiously. The young man has just become an intern, and is anxious to have his father see him, for the first time, in intern's uniform. He feels proud, perhaps a bit vain. He is called to the phone, picks it up, says hello. His face undergoes a sudden change; he turns pale, tears stream down his cheeks. He has learned of his father's death—of his father run over on the sidewalk by a truck. He turns away from the phone, seeing nothing in front of him, and stumbles away. He is still sobbing.

I was that intern.
The man was my father.

My world seemed to be over after this; I wondered if I would ever get over the shock, if I would ever recover from the horror. I ate little, slept less, felt bitterness fester inside me. I felt tired and depressed, even walking seemed an effort, my thoughts were sometimes incoherent. For months I lost contact with reality and retreated from the world of people and pain.

Finally, I realized that I had to continue with my life and with my work. Even though my father would never see me as an intern or a doctor, I had to vindicate all the years of struggle he went through for me.

I began to see my friends again; I learned to laugh again. I picked up the pieces and put them together. I renounced spiritual suicide and once more began to live for each day.

This is what we all must do in life. We must survive misfortune, survive uncertainty, pick ourselves off the floor, and go back to creative living.

But you need a friend at times like this, your self-image, for a proper self-image is the powerhouse within you that enables you to stand up under stress.

Indeed, the power of your self-image, intangible as it is, can outdistance the uncertainties with which you may wrestle.

Many people would feel ruined if what happened to golfer Ben Hogan happened to them. At the top of his game, Hogan, as many will recall, almost lost his life in a terrible auto crash. Few conceived the possibility that he would ever play top echelon golf again. Yet Ben Hogan had a faith in himself that enabled him to overcome such a horrifying experience. Not only did he return to golf, but he returned as a champion.

Would you still be playing football if you were Jerry Kramer of the professional Green Bay Packers? He has been operated on for a chipped vertebra in the neck region and has played this violent game with a broken ankle. Three weeks after a huge splinter pierced his groin and tore through his abdomen, Kramer was back in football uniform. With a detached retina and with a shotgun wound, he has played blockbusting football. Once he was hurled from a car going 100 miles an hour. The car, smashing into a tree, rolled over Kramer and erupted in flames. Kramer got to his feet, undaunted, ready for new experiences. To the best of my knowledge, he is still knocking down opponents for the Green Bay Packers. He has more than his 250-odd pounds of muscle going for him; he has belief in himself.

Let me tell you another story. This one is about war, and nothing is more uncertain than war—especially if you're in the frontline infantry.

War and Dentistry

This friend of mine was drafted into the Army during World War II and was shipped to Europe a few months after D-day, a rifleman in an infantry company. In Alsace-Lorraine he first saw action against the Germans.

He was at the front about six months, emerging as one of a handful of survivors in a company of about two hundred men. He rose through the ranks from private to staff sergeant, was recommended for decorations three different times, received one medal for heroism. He led many patrols at night behind the German lines, went first in countless attacks on fortified enemy positions, escaped death more than once by inches.

Once, in a large town near the German border, he knocked out an enemy machine gun and saved a wounded man's life, carrying him to safety.

Another time his lieutenant, during a midnight patrol behind the German lines, called on him to take his squad through barbed wire and mine fields to capture prisoners for Intelligence. He went first, seized four prisoners from a house, and the information they revealed may have helped defeat a massive German counterattack.

On patrol again he took his squad across a bridge into a lone house on the outskirts of a small village. At dusk a German was killed storming the doorway.

He and his men spent the night in the house separated from their comrades across the bridge, the decaying corpse in the doorway. My friend's quiet courage kept his men calm during the terrifying night when all feared they might be surrounded and killed.

Once he was foolhardly and got away with it. He went back with a buddy from their outpost in a house—they were in a town just over the German border—to a beer factory they had bypassed the day before. The two hoisted a huge beer barrel on their shoulders and crawled back through the streets of this town, infested with snipers and barraged by German 88 artillery pieces, to bring the beer to their comrades.

Anyway, he survived the war. Frightened, naturally, he was nevertheless able to control his fears and to assume leadership while others were breaking down under the mounting strain.

Does it surprise you that a fellow who has known such danger and uncertainty is terrified of the dentist? that he finds it difficult to work the day before he has a dental appointment— even for a cleaning or the filling of a small cavity? that he grips the arms of the dental chair desperately even at the *sound* of the drill beginning to hum? that he breaks out in a cold sweat when the drilling starts?

How do you explain this?

Self-image.

At the front he felt accepting of himself, was proud of his role, was therefore able to endure the ordeals he had to face.

In the dental chair he feels ashamed of his fear, which he knows is unjustified; his image of himself shrinks.

I find this a fascinating story because it gets right to the heart of the basic truth which I will pound home to you again and again: it is the strength of your self-image which, by and large, will determine whether or not you can overcome your obstacles. Realistic uncertainties may be unpleasant factors now and then, but you can live with any danger if you are with yourself all the way.

As life gets faster, with discotheques springing up all around you, rock 'n' roll music jangling your nerves, swerving cars almost dismembering you as you cross the street, and jets thundering overhead, you must turn to your self-image for your certainty. You must rely on your image of yourself; you must build it every chance you get.

Here's an exercise that will help you.

Exercise 1

Each day, several times a day, when you are shaving or applying lipstick, brushing your teeth or washing your face, look at yourself in the mirror. Any mirror will do, as long as it is unbroken and unclouded; the main idea is that you get a good look at yourself.

Take stock of your physical image. Don't run to your next hustle-bustle activity of the day: stay awhile and look. After you are finished with your brushing or washing or whatever, stay a few minutes more and get reacquainted with your face.

Why reacquainted? Because chances are, if your mind is a spinning jumble of worries, you have forgotten the nature of your real physical image. You have lost it. You have lost it to obsessive fears, to anxieties, to depression. You may easily image faces which threaten you: perhaps your boss's or a competitor who beats you out for things or a policeman who made you feel guilty while he wrote out a ticket for some minor traffic violation. But your own image, have you lost it? If your self-image is weak, you doubtless have.

However, I must first make one thing clear: *This is not meant to be an exercise in self-love; the encouragement of narcissism will do you only harm.* Do not look at yourself and tell yourself that you are perfect, that you are better than other people! This would be a distortion and would only earn for your enemies or people who laughed at your foolishness.

This mirror-gazing is a rescue operation: it is a rescuing of your physical image from the avalanche of life forces which can submerge it. You are reviving your physical image of yourself; as I will show you, you will also revive your interconnected emotional image of yourself, and we will tie them together into a realistic, integrated picture of what you are, a human being trying to do his best for himself and others in a world full of avenues for rich, creative living.

As you look at yourself in the mirror, do not let yourself fall prey to the opposite of narcissism: destructive self-criticism. Your features may not be perfect; do not expect perfection. Accept your image as it is.

Your purpose is self-discovery—or self-rediscovery. Untangle yourself from the web of anxieties and tensions that whirl around in your brain, break free from the frightened-child feelings which grip you, *and just look at your face for awhile.* For it is the face of a person who has lived through experiences and achieved successes—few perhaps, minor perhaps, but successes.

See the person behind the face, the human being behind the face. Look at yourself realistically, and keep this image of yourself alive—but be good to yourself and look into your treasure-box of experiences for your successes, for your good moments, for your winning feelings.

Our astronauts have orbited around the earth for days and days, and then have come back. You orbit every day around your self-image; your lifeline is attached to it. When you venture forth into the world of people and things, if your self-image is strong, you will feel at home in this world —even with its dangers and uncertainties. You will retreat only if your image of yourself is a poor one and, therefore, people's opinions of you upset you.

There is much commotion about outer space these days, but surely it is obvious that the "inner space" within your mind is what is important to you. Do not doubt the imperativeness of this exploration into "inner space."

See yourself realistically, physically, emotionally; see in your mind, then, your successful experiences in life; picture them over and over and over until they become part of you.

Every day look at yourself, physically, and in your mind, and work to strengthen your image of yourself, always working to strengthen this "inner space" of your mind.

Make every day a voyage of discovery into this "inner space." You can count down from ten to zero and ask yourself: "How is my self-image today?"

Symbolically, you are on a bicycle moving forward. Don't drive backward. There is only one kind of creative retreat; a permanent retreat from past mistakes, failure, griefs. Cut the umbilical cord now from past distresses; let the past get lost in the orbit of time. Living means going forward whether you are aware of it or not, whether you like it or not. Go into orbit in life; don't retreat into empty space.

As you look into your mirror, tell yourself that you will go forward, that you will not passively submit to the opinion of others, but that you will be with yourself, face-to-face with yourself, strengthening yourself, supporting yourself.

It is this sense of self that will help you to live creatively.

Every day take advantage of your few minutes in front of a mirror to get closer to yourself in the sensible way I have described, and you will be building the self-image which you need for resourceful living.

The Need for Inner Certainty

You must develop this inner certainty because the external world will always have its dangers. You can survive them if you strengthen your feeling of self.

I know of a man who fled from the Nazis halfway across Europe, who spent three years in the shadow of death, who is today a successful salesman and father of three fine children.

I know of another man, a young man, who escaped through the Iron Curtain and, after many terrifying experiences, finally went to England, and then to the United States, where he is now doing well as an expert in refrigeration.

How would you like it if you moved your family of four from your apartment to another apartment miles away? Just as you had finished unpacking, your company offered you a promotion on condition that you move immediately to another state. I know of a young fellow this happened to; it didn't throw him. He accepted the enormous inconvenience, told his wife they were moving again, and he did well in his new job.

What about women? Each time a woman becomes pregnant, accepts the responsibilities of motherhood, she is also accepting the uncertainties of fate. What will her child be like? How will it look? Will it be normal? Boy or girl? Like father or like mother? How will her unborn child make out in life?

Many years ago a friend of mine, a famous novelist in her fifties, was in an auto accident. She came to see me in my office; she was in a terrible panic. I succeeded in calming her somewhat.

Then I said to her, "Listen, dear, you've lived through a rough experience. You're on a fence now, but you can't stay there. You have to jump to one side or the other. Which side do you want to jump to, the side of fear, negation, frustration—or the creative, positive, useful side? It's not easy for you now, I know, but you have to decide."

She was able to pull herself together; she assumed her former life-going role in the world; she had enough respect for herself to rise above the frightening experience.

I lectured in Denver, Colorado, not too long ago. After I finished, a man of about seventy came up to me. "Your talk was very instructive, Doctor—perfect for younger people. But I've lived my life, I'm on borrowed time. What can it do for me?"

I said, "Everyone is on borrowed time, whether seven or seventy. Every day is a lifetime. Living means that you must live each day to the full—to forget your past errors and disappointments and your future uncertainties. Start living right now; do your best and accept your best; you have no right to give up on life!"

The Road to Happy Living

Life holds many surprises for us, not all pleasant, and the person who would live creatively in today's world must develop a strong self-image.

You cannot rely on "luck," and you cannot base your life on the opinions of other people. You must do it yourself, and you must do it in a world full of frustrations and dangers.

You must constantly work to improve your mental image of yourself, to feel better about yourself. You can do this if you are willing to work hard, without preconceptions of magical solutions, following the suggestions I will offer you in this book.

Each day you have many occasions to look into a mirror; when you brush your teeth, when you shave or powder your nose, when you comb your hair, when you wash your face.

Go beyond these simple, useful functions and use the mirror to help you to become reacquainted with the outer image of a self you may have lost sight of in the rushing pace of life today. Learn to accept this physical image of yourself and the inner self behind it; we will discuss the principles underlying such self-acceptance in the following chapters.

You must recover your sense of self. Many people have lost this sense and do not understand that they have lost it—or the sorrowful consequences of this loss.

You must understand this: You can have an expensive house, two cars, a sizable bank account, own stocks and real estate, and still feel poor—if you have lost touch with a wholesome image-sense of yourself.

If you feel poor, then uncertainties will frighten you, and you will find them all around you.

Pliny the Elder, the famous Roman writer, once commented that "The only certainty is that nothing is certain."

But life's perils need not worry you; they need not keep you from full living.

Not if you feel that you are a worthwhile person.

You must be able to allow yourself joy. You must feel at one with yourself.

Then a sense of security will replace worry, and you will be able to live happily with a minimum of uncertainty.

The Power in Life Activities

How DO YOU spend your day?

The minutes and hours that tick away on your wristwatch, are they your opportunity or your burden?

Do you say to yourself, "Oh, it's so early in the day! How will I kill the next few hours?"

Or do you move toward life activities, bristling and eager, seeking new adventures, mastering new mechanisms or concepts, understanding more about your human fellows? Time moves too fast for you; you cannot get enough minutes and hours to encompass your interests in the world.

"Life" is a misleading word because people do so many things with it. The person who broods in self-pity and vegetates while others pass him by is only half-alive. If you are like this, don't feel ashamed—you have millions and millions of people for company—but understand that you must try to change so that you have a chance to know what happiness is.

For there is happiness, there is power, in life activities. There is strength and joy in going forward toward other people, toward the processes around which civilization has fastened its approval or its permissiveneess. This may seem an obvious point to make, but often we lose sight of the most elemental truths and this can cost us greatly in terms of suffering.

When you wake up in the morning, you must alert yourself to the day ahead, to the possibilities for joyful living that the coming hours will bring if you use them fully. The things you do during this day may not shake *the* world, but they may make *your* world.

I know of a fellow who would swear by a hearty breakfast, to "start the day full of energy." He would stow away six or eight eggs, three or four bowls of cereal, ten or twelve pieces of toast, and wash it down with several glasses of milk and three or four cups of coffee. The results in his case were dubious: he developed a big stomach, but he did have one good idea—start the day right, get energy to live.

Unfortunately, however, many people are passive to life and withdraw from its pleasures. It is this movement-away-from-life that I would like to see reversed; it is this renunciation of people's creative potentials that I would like to see exposed as absurd.

When you want to, go fishing and lap up the sunshine. But do it actively, not passively.

Otherwise, even the fish will say, "I won't bite. Can't you move about a little more?"

My advice to you, you people who go from bed to television set to newspaper to movie house to restaurant to bed is: There is more to life than being passive. There are great things that you can do every day; open your eyes to them.

The Joy of Productive Work

First let us consider the hysterical flight from work at about five o'clock each day, a flight as urgent as one from an approaching hurricane or from a Martian invasion. Is work such a scourge? Is it as deadly as a boa constrictor, its coils winding about you, squeezing you to death?

Many people nowadays seem to think so. Work is like an alarm clock to them; they are clock-watchers who cannot wait for the signal to get away.

I disagree, emphatically, with this concept. I think that productive work is one of the true goods of life; when you work productively, you manufacture more than money, you also manufacture a sense of self-esteem for yourself.

The Scottish essayist-historian Thomas Carlyle wrote: "Blessed is he who has found his work; let him ask no other blessedness . . . Even in the meanest sorts of Labor, the whole soul of a man is composed into a kind of real harmony the instant he sets himself to work."

I have not always agreed with Carlyle, but I can second

these words from my own experience. I have known people functioning harmoniously in the world of work whose souls shriveled when they lost or gave up their jobs. Even their faces changed; indifference was in their eyes where once there had been excitement.

It is true that some people work at jobs ill-suited to them; their work is enslavement because they do not enjoy it. They work only for the money. They do not feel the exultation of a person who pours his most productive powers into his work.

If this is your situation, you must think about remedying it because your chances for creative living are slim if you feel dead in your work.

Perhaps you haven't given your job the attention it deserves. Perhaps you haven't opened your eyes completely to the potentialities around you. Perhaps you are not aware of the fact that you, and not the job, might be at fault. Try to remember that, in many instances, you create the opportunity, not your job.

If your job is at fault, you must then find for yourself another line of work if you possibly can; even a small cut in pay may be worthwhile if you are able to switch to work which makes you feel more alive. If this is not possible, you may sublimate your work productivity in enriching hobbies.

Never withdraw from productive work into inertia. You are a human being, not a mattress, and you should utilize your human resources all your life to attain a feeling of completeness.

You must plan now for the future. Think about what activities you will be doing later on when you retire or when your work becomes less demanding.

I am over sixty-five and long ago, realizing that my days as a plastic surgeon would not last forever, I began to study the craft of writing. I talked to writers and editors and publishers and read books on writing. Then I began to write books. Today I spend half my work time practicing plastic surgery, the other half writing. When I am seventy-five, I will still be working—mostly as a writer. This is how much I value work that I love.

I feel as productive as I've ever felt, and this makes me

feel good. I continue to enjoy fully my interconnection with the world.

There is joy in work that you love to do; there is growth in it.

Leo Tolstoy once wrote that man's happiness in living is involved in his work.

This is so true.

Your Time Is Yours to Enjoy

When you finish your work, you will have the gift of time, but what will you do with this gift? Chances are your hours are shorter than they used to be—even if you are a housewife. So you will have more time to enjoy yourself.

"But," you may say, "I don't know what to do with my time. It is a terrible problem."

This is not correct. If you feel this way, *time* is not your problem. *You* are the problem.

You must see this, and then you must do something about it. It makes no sense to throw away a gift.

Sometimes a small child, in a fit of temper, will destroy a genuinely loved object. But, if you are reading this book, I assume that you are not a small child. Childhood has long since passed; the period of experimentation is over, and those trial-and-error days will not return. You must now know what you're doing. You have tools at your command. One is the wisdom, the sense of values gained from your years of living. Surely you must see the preciousness of your free time.

In the words of Benjamin Franklin, "Dost thou love life? Then do not squander time, for that is the stuff life is made of."

You must learn to use this life-stuff, to fill it with active living—not with boredom, apathy, resignation. Would you empty your wallet or pocketbook into a trash can? Then why throw away time, which is also valuable?

You must learn to use time energetically, productively, to enhance your feeling of true participation in and enjoyment of the life process.

You can channel your time into all kinds of stimulating areas.

You must realize that leisure time is just as important as work time. You are a whole person, not just a working machine, and you and you alone have the opportunity within you to keep yourself whole.

Leisure time may mean many things—sports, painting, cooking, card games, gardening, and a host of other activities. You must realize that leisure belongs to you, like your eyes, like your heart. Take it. You and you alone must find one aspect of leisure that will help you reach self-fulfillment.

Take a look at yourself in the mirror—ask yourself, without playing games, who you are and what you are doing with yourself. This self-confrontation requires an answer. You can't be on the fence of indecision. Once you honestly make a response, you will find the activities that will make you happy.

And when you do, play to the full . . . concentrate creatively on the activity. No one can do it for you. When you play tennis, *play* tennis. When you are gardening, garden as if it is for the moment the most important thing in your life.

I must warn you that concentration is a process that can be done creatively only if you learn to do one thing at a time—and you learn to do it well before you take on another challenge. Concentration does not mean exhausting yourself with too many activities all at once. Choose one and master that. Then go on to another. You'll find great satisfaction from these leisure-time activities which you have made a part of your new creative life.

A good rule for both work and leisure time is to set a goal for yourself each and every day.

A Goal Every Day

Since this is so important and it lies at the foundation of my theories on psycho-cybernetics and self-image psychology, I have devoted a full chapter later on in this book to the need for goals, but I will mention it here.

To enjoy yourself, you must have goals. Living is a series

of goals and the question is, do you achieve them or are you frustrated—do you gain pleasure or is pain the result?

Many people understand the importance of goals in living but are too harsh in their demands upon themselves. They feel that their goals are too insignificant, that since their achievements will hardly speed the enactment of total nuclear disarmament or end all racial prejudice, these goals are not worthwhile.

This is a mistake. While you might not be President Johnson, making decisions of global importance; or Richard Rodgers, working on a new musical which millions may see; or Mickey Mantle, whose home runs carry 450 feet; you are an individual also, you too are made in God's image and endowed with a wonderful body; you too have a mind, feelings, needs, aspirations; you too mean something—*if you mean something to yourself*.

If you are a teen-ager, there is no shortage of goals for you. Choosing a vocation, mastering a skill, exploring an alien subject matter, hitting a baseball, learning a popular dance, making new friends, meeting a congenial mate. And, within the span of these broad goals, you can pinpoint daily goals that are satisfying for you.

If you are in your twenties, thirties or forties, your broader goals may change in terms of specifics, but they are nonetheless potentially satisfying. You may be involved in enlarging your vocational scope, raising a family, managing money skillfully, learning hobbies. From day to day, you too may aim at achievements within the framework of these larger goals—or simply at spur-of-the-moment things that are fun.

You should think in terms of daily goals, too, not just life goals.

If you are older, cooking a good meal for yourself and your husband is a fine goal; it may be commonplace, but it is productive. You give him satisfaction with your labor and, the more creatively you work with your ingredients, the more pleasure you give him—and yourself.

Painting a picture may give many people days of enjoyment—even weeks. Mixing the paints, organizing your materials, brushing on your colors, shading and shaping for subtle effects. It's not Rembrandt? That's not the point. Are you putting the best you have into the picture? Is it more imaginative or more vivid or more daring than *your* last picture? Would you like to frame it and hang it in your living room? No? Well maybe the bedroom this time. Next try, the living room. It's more important to you than the next flight into outer space. And it should be.

You must not block yourself off from your goals. You must move every day, feel a sense of direction toward a goal every day, no matter how small that goal may be. You keep moving in the stream of things, doing the best you can. And if you have no goal, you keep moving anyway—and a goal will catch up with you. Your sense of direction is forward.

Recently a woman consulted me about removing some wrinkles from her face. She wondered if she was doing the right thing coming to my office without letting her family know.

"Why didn't you tell them?" I asked.

"They'd be against it. My husband and married daughter would think me vain and foolish."

I said that in my many years of practice as a plastic surgeon I never saw a case of out-and-out vanity: that people seek the aid of the plastic surgeon for psychological, social, and economic reasons. They want their defect removed because they want a second chance in life.

She said, "That's it, Doctor. I do want a second chance. I want to look my best for my family."

"Explain it to them," I suggested.

Later I operated on this lady; while she was in the hospital, she confessed that she hadn't been able to speak to her husband. The operation was entirely successful, but her husband was furious, unforgiving.

Too often people block attempts at movement—as this woman's husband did. Internal wrinkles, deeper than facial wrinkles, remain. Plastic surgery will not remove these inner wrinkles; only forgiveness will.

The Pleasure in Doing

While I was organizing my material for this chapter, a letter came in the mail from Houston, Texas. I read it and felt pleased.

It was from two women who had read my book *Psycho-Cybernetics* and set about applying its principles. They wrote that I had opened new areas of possibilities for them, allowing them to attempt projects which they had never before dared to consider.

Since realizing that their limitations in action were largely limitations which only they could impose on themselves, they freed themselves to:

write a children's book (in the bookstores)

write a screen treatment

write the first five chapters of a mystery novel

form a corporation

think up two games which they are about to market.

All this, they wrote, in less than a year.

"We both have full-time jobs," they added.

"Don't tell us to slow down; we're having the time of our lives. . . . If stuck, we program—and out comes the answer. . . . With all this, we thought you deserved a word of thanks."

These women set goals for themselves, knocked over unrealistic inhibitions that kept them from attacking them, felt their worth strongly enough to push forward, and then let their success mechanisms work for them within the range of their creative abilities.

You need not set as many goals or be as ambitious in the caliber of your goals as these two women, but you must recognize the success thrust in you and seek to free it, not block it.

God did not put you on this earth to languish in misery; He gave you success impulses. You must use them.

If you have problems, if you meet obstacles, then you're just like most people. Most of you are familiar with the life story of Helen Keller, who overcame staggering physical handicaps to rise to her incredible achievements. You may not know that Florence Nightingale, the famed nurse, was a confirmed hypochondriac whose services of mercy involved convincing herself first that *she* was not dying.

If you learn to believe in yourself, and do what you want to do, your accomplishments may amaze you.

People Can Be More Fun for You

Are people fun for you—or do you find them boring? Do you try to relate to people—or do you avoid involvement?

Your relations with other people constitute one of the fundamental facets of your life. These relations are complex; many people underestimate their complexity. There is so much need to improve the caliber of our friendships. What finer goal for part of every day? What could have greater meaning?

There is room for much growth in this area of inter-personal relating. Among people today, endless problems stand in the way of true friendliness: conflicting self-interest, inhibition, resentment based on nothing, inability to listen, egocentric attitudes, grudge-holding of years' duration, intolerance toward individual differences. I could extend this catalogue for another page of solid type, listing the many elements that keep people from friendly communication with each other.

I do not believe in obscuring the truth. If there is anything I have observed in the relations of human beings, it is our tendency toward friction—more often subtle than direct. There is much inner hurt, secret misunderstanding, preconceived nonsense; there are emotional scars that heal slowly—if at all. None of us is immune from making mistakes with other people, and it's nothing to be ashamed of; I've made my mistakes, too.

You must not withdraw from people when you feel hurt. Instead, think actively of ways you can improve your sensitive relationships. What a joy when you do! One's capacity for friendship, which can be developed, is basic to one's capacity for happiness.

You can make this art of friendship one of the greatest

goals in your life. As a matter of fact, it must be the greatest goal in your life.

Basic to anything, however, no matter what your circumstances, is your attitude toward yourself.

Happiness in Your Self-Image

To a great degree you are what you think you are and you can do what you think you can do. Your attitude toward yourself gives you a lift or pushes you into despair.

Your self-image, this is what gives you joy or heartbreak, success or failure, happiness or pain.

Your self-image can help you to do what you must to enjoy your work, and it can help you to enjoy your play. It can give you confidence in your work and in the activities which you choose for your leisure time.

Resolve to be joyful: to be charitable in your self-appraisals, to see yourself in your best moments, to strengthen this pleasant vision of yourself—based on reality, not myth, but on a positive picture of reality.

While a person who has had wholesome help in his formative years will find the maintenance of a healthy self-image possible with no effort at all, still, with effort and understanding, I feel that anyone can strengthen this mental picture of himself to the extent that life is tolerable, even rewarding. Then, with repeated effort, with compassion for his limitations, with endless striving to bring forth the image of himself that is uplifting—and everyone has *some* good moments —he can continue to consolidate his gains in self-esteem.

Two ideas which will never let you down:

1. Set goals every day you live.
2. Never withdraw from life.

A Young Spirit in an Old Body

Recently, on a lecture tour, I visited the West Coast. I went to San Diego and then by plane to San Francisco. Seated next to me on the plane was a lady of eighty-six, and we talked to each other. She was of English extraction and told me how she had founded a home for older English people in California, not far from Pasadena. At eighty-six she still visits the home every day as a sort of "President Emeritus" and also finds time to attend meetings of a club she helped create, devoted to the interests of older people.

"I am active every day," she told me.

"Do you find that your age handicaps you?" I asked.

"I don't think about my age. I enjoy myself and I try to make each day exciting. I like to talk, and I like to listen too."

"You are a very youthful eighty-six."

"Every day is interesting to me," she answered. She was no hypocrite; her eyes sparkled with life.

After a few days in San Francisco, I boarded the plane to return to San Diego. En route we stopped at Santa Barbara where fifty youngsters, aged about nine to fifteen, got on the plane, accompanied by their instructors. An instructor told me this was a club for delinquents, boys who ran away from home or who committed petty crimes; they were on probation.

This time my seat-mate was a boy of about twelve. Though young, his eyes were dull, reflecting whatever frustrations he had lived through in his brief life, whatever clouds had blurred his self-image.

He turned away from me and spent the entire trip looking through the airplane window. When we circled over San Diego, he made his only observation. "I see people down below. They look like bugs."

The remark in someone else could have been innocent, perhaps, but in this sad boy with the dead eyes I could feel that the comparison of people with bugs had meaning. To him people were nasty creatures; his self-image was weak, and he could admit no virtues in others. He saw life as futile. I felt sorry for the young fellow and hoped that the guidance he received in the club would help him to find the positive qualities in himself that he could not see.

I could not help comparing the eagerness of the eighty-six-year-old lady with the listlessness of the twelve-year-old boy. It is not age that dulls people's lives; it is emotional blockage.

The Barbershop Quartet

In San Diego I went to a barbershop to have my shoes shined. I sat down and listened to the talk around me. A quartet of men were singing the praises of their cars.

"I have a Chevy, a beauty. It's done close to 30,000 miles and no trouble."

"Mine's done over 40,000."

"How often do you get the oil changed?"

"Oh, I don't know, maybe every 2,000 miles. How about you?"

"I don't think that's enough, pal. I get mine changed every 1,000 miles. Filter every 3,000 to 5,000. That's the way you keep your car in good shape."

"I don't know. My car's done over 60,000, and I change the oil maybe every 1,200 or 1,300 miles."

"You take care of your car, it'll take care of you."

The four men kept talking, two getting haircuts, two cutting their hair. The shoeshine fellow and I just listened.

I had to think to myself: "These fellows seem to know cars —and there's nothing wrong with that—but do they know anything at all about their self-image? They look to be about thirty-five to forty-five, all of them, but do they ever think of creative living? They like to be good citizens; they are well shaved, they keep their hair cut neatly, they oil their cars, they probably spend their Sunday mornings washing their cars down so that the metal sparkles. Their cars will certainly get them to their destinations, but do they believe in other positive goals for each day? Do they see a glistening self-image, or have they lost it in their fight for money and status and in their exclusive absorption in cars and such?"

George Bernard Shaw once counseled his readers to keep their souls clean, comparing them to windows through which they could then see the life around them.

What sound thinking! But most of us, regrettably, take better care of our cars than we do of our image of ourselves, which disappears somewhere—and, with it, our drive for happiness.

The Strength Is an Active Philosophy

In our difficult world there are many easy solutions—but these solutions are not always the best ones.

If you are bored, you may spend your spare time engulfed in a combination of television-radio-movies-phonograph records—but wouldn't you feel better if you actively tackled some project, some hobby, something to which you committed your creative zest?

If you are lazy, you can stick a precooked dinner in the oven—but perhaps you might have cooked a better meal yourself, and enjoyed the living involved in doing this chore.

You can even spend your day resting on your bed, all alone, sealed off from life—but couldn't you do better?

Needless to say, I'm not against television, movies, radio, phonograph records or precooked dinners—nor am I against resting—in moderation.

What I am against is an essentially passive way of doing things. When you are passive, you retire from the excitement of life and the enjoyment of stimulating give-and-take. You move away from the life process; you kill life in yourself. Yet life can invade you, can inflict suffering on you, while you lie helplessly, passively, a victim of your own inertia.

"I am in debt," you say, "and I have to save my energy for making money."

"Does being a spectator help you?"

"Well, I don't know, but . . ."

Yes, you may have financial problems, most people do, but a boring life will not stimulate you to overcome them.

"How about X?" you say. "He's only forty-five, and he just had a heart attack last week and . . ."

"That's too bad about X; I'm sorry to hear it and I'm sure you're sorry, too."

But it will not help you to bore yourself to death, worrying, apprehensively listening to your heartbeat.

Your strength is not in the premature burial of your participation in life; it is in your pursuance of an active philosophy—in optimistic, realistic, active living.

Do, create, innovate.

Stay in the world, and do not baby yourself.

Do you remember the story of the female aviator Amelia Earhart? She was the first great woman flier, the first of her sex to fly across the Atlantic Ocean. She loved airplanes, loved flying so much that she put off marriage for several years so that she could get her fill. Congress presented her with the Distinguished Flying Cross, and in the 1930's her name was on everyone's lips. She was feted, dined, deluged with fan mail; she broke flying records, delivered lectures, wrote articles.

Finally, she started out on a flight around the world in 1937. Her plane just disappeared. There was worldwide interest, but search parties failed to find her. What happened we will probably never know, but in all probability Amelia Earhart died before reaching the age of forty.

Terrible misfortune to a great doer, but a person like this, who goes and does and lives and enjoys, lives more in a short lifetime than someone with a life span of 100 who mopes and dozes and never gets his feet wet.

While you live, this is the way to live—like an Amelia Earhart.

Do, work, cook, paint, write, talk, argue, sew, play the piano, read, think, walk, dance, play checkers, play bridge. Do. You know what you like to do: do it!

You're a terrible bridge player? You pushed your partner to seven no-trump with one point in your hand? Well, I'm glad I'm not your partner, and I hope you're not playing for money, but if you're feeling the pleasure of playing cards, this is infinitely more worthwhile than lying on your bed, fretting, looking at the ceiling—even if your bridge partner gave you a very dirty look.

You've found a choral group and joined it? You love to sing? Good! But you can't carry a tune? If it means something to you, practice your singing; maybe a friend will help you. If you can't improve, perhaps the choral group will tolerate your discordant voice—just because they like you.

You don't have to be perfect, but you do have to take part, you do have to be involved. The stronger your self-

estimate, the better, but regardless you do have to remain
in the "mainstream" of life.

God created life in us so that we could live actively in
the world He fashioned. God made us, with our marvelous
bodies and our complex minds, so that we could have meaning and happiness in our lives.

If you believe in a Higher Power, you must believe in
the purpose in life, no matter how difficult the world may
seem during depressing periods.

Tear fear from your heart; bury your negative thinking!
tell off friends who try to convince you that life is dull.

Exercise 2

One of the biggest obstacles to your setting of your daily
goals will be fear of failure. You may decide to play it safe;
if you try nothing, especially nothing new, then you will
not blunder.

At this point you must help yourself; you must be a
friend to yourself.

Arrange yourself so that you are comfortable. Seat yourself in a plush armchair or, if you prefer, lie down on a
couch or pace the floor. You know what will make *you* feel
primed to think.

Then reason with yourself. Everyone needs to do this;
there is no person, and never has been a person, who is
always reasonable.

Ask yourself why you must be so perfect. Have you ever
met a perfect mother? a perfect father? a perfect teacher?
a perfect salesman? a perfect citizen? a perfect driver? Ex-
cellent, maybe—but perfect?

Then why should you expect such unattainable perfection
from yourself?

If you are afraid to set goals for yourself, reason with
yourself along these lines. Do it every day. You will feel
better for it, I feel confident.

Do not be afraid to make mistakes. When you start your
day and set your goals, tell yourself, "I may be a mistake-
maker, but I am also a mistake-breaker."

You will become a "mistake-breaker" when you live each

day courageously and bend your important little world to your will—as much as you can, and in a constructive, co-operative spirit.

And this positive performance will help you achieve your goals—will actually enhance your possibilities of success and happiness.

Stop blocking yourself from your goals!

Start living.

• 4 •

Dynamic Living Starts *NOW*

JUST AS WE get into the habit of doing things without questioning—buttoning a shirt, brushing our teeth, washing the dishes—so we tend to adopt culturally stereotyped ways of thinking without making a real individual selection. Often we may uncritically accept patterns of thought which do not make real sense.

About creative living, for example. I think most people believe it is silly to devote time to thinking about creative living. One's life pattern is either dynamic or static; planning will not help.

I disagree.

I believe, firmly, that sound planning plants the seeds of rich, dynamic living.

In rising above the animal state, man increasingly has used planning to achieve the goals he values, most of which are not spur-of-the-moment accomplishments.

The forty-two-year-old doctor, with his comfortable practice, will have figured out his lifework perhaps in his early teens, as a high school student.

The lawyer and the physicist, too, doing work they like and receiving rewarding pay for their efforts, paved the way for their successes with similar planning.

The incomparable inventor Thomas Edison—about

whom we shall have much to say—was experimenting with his mechanical environment when he was six years old.

Many of our timeless entertainers, such as Donald O'Connor, performed as children and enlarged their talents through experience and experimentation.

Years of balanced creative living, these, too, must be anticipated. Plan them when you are young, middle-aged, or in your later years—but start planning now.

When you are in high school, in college, starting your first job, raising your children, building your career, cultivating your mature ideas, visiting your grandchildren—during these years, you should be going beyond your function, always looking to fill your years with life.

The essential ingredient in your plans must be the development of your belief in yourself as a human being *in* the world, not outside it, living each day fully, not fleeing in fear from the demands of life.

The search from childhood to old age is the search for a healthy self-image. Fearful of approaching the threshold of adult life, we search for it during adolescence. We seek to strengthen it during adult life and spend a lifetime in this pursuit—if we are wise and if we do not lose it in paying homage to false gods and worthless values. If we are sensible, we continue to build on it during our later years instead of finding the easy way out in a passive withdrawal from life.

All people must realize that they must live fully today. They must understand that each day is a lifetime to be lived *now* and that the mistakes of yesterday must be left in the tomb of time. The young become mature and the mature become young when they learn to deal with negative feelings and to rise through them to their full recognition of themselves as adequate human beings.

This is not an oversimplification; anything else is an overcomplication of something that is really simple.

You must learn to accept yourself now in realistic terms. This is basic.

I do not mean that you should constantly tell yourself how wonderful you are, how much better you are than anyone else. Once again, this is a narcissistic process of going away from oneself into a world of fantasy. Your estimate of yourself must be valid and must take into consideration your fellows around you; aspiring to see yourself in your best moments and trying to prolong and extend these moments, you must also honestly see your weaknesses and be compassionate toward them, as you would be compassionate toward the weaknesses of a loved friend.

My point is that you must, at as early an age as possible, feel good enough about yourself so that you need not run away from life. You must get into the habit of accepting yourself, in the world, in life, without retreat—even if you find no perfection.

If you truly accept yourself and the world you live in, you are laying the groundwork for dynamic living.

This is the only solid base for real living.

Orange Drinks and Cigars

Let me give you an example of how not to develop a strong self-image.

When I was seventeen, I got my first job, dispensing orange drinks at Coney Island in Brooklyn during the hot summer months.

It was hot and one customer never stopped drinking— me.

Whenever there was slack business, I would hide behind the dispensing bar and ladle myself up some more orange drink.

In spite of my dilution of profits, I earned $8.00 the first week. A few pounds heavier, the liquid swirling inside me as I walked, I went to a candy store and bought a large box of five-cent cigars.

I smoked cigar after cigar—until I got nauseous. Someone had to help me get home. There I threw up a few times, looked with horror at my pale face in the mirror, and stumbled to bed where I tossed and turned all night.

What is the point of this little story?

It is not an attack on cigars. I smoke cigars today, and I enjoy them.

My point is that at the time I was not used to cigars

and did not like them; I had never smoked one before, and they were no part of my life. But I had an image of what I should be like; I should look like a successful, cigar-smoking he-man. So, bloated with a feeling of power in my ridiculous fantasy, I smoked cigar after cigar, basking in the glow of my unrealistic image of myself—until it all went up in smoke.

And I became sick.

If taken in a symbolic sense, this story exemplifies the harm one can do to oneself by fleeing from his true nature as a human being into a world of fantasy—or of retirement from life, for that matter.

At no age in life can you afford to be ignorant of the true nature of yourself; at no age can you afford to turn away from your true self-image with disrespect. You will do injury to yourself if you act in ways that you think other people expect you to act, if these ways run contrary to the fiber of your being.

A Girl in a Boy's World

Now let me tell you another story, one which comes back to me from the faraway world of my childhood.

It's about "Wingy," the president of our gang of boys, our leader—although she was a girl.

It's about Wingy, who never gave up on life, who never gave up on herself.

Growing up in the jungle streets of the Lower East Side in New York City, my friends and I learned to savor its noisy delights and to avoid its overcrowded perils. Wagons and carts spun down the narrow, tenement-lined streets; quick on our feet, we would dart between the huge wheels, escaping injury as part of our daily life.

Our childhood on those crowded streets had many joys. We would dive blissfully into the orange-and-melon-infested waters of the East River, surfacing to see some enormous ship churning downstream. We would parade down close-packed Attorney Street, and sometimes the pushcart vendors would give us leftovers from the food they had been selling. Our gang was a beehive of loud arguments—about nothing, perhaps, but loud, fun.

But the carts could be dangerous.

We regarded dodging their wheels as male sport, but Wingy insisted on joining us. This was before we made her a member of our club; at this time we tried to avoid her.

One day Wingy was dodging the wheels of a horsedrawn beer wagon when a terrified dog came bounding up, causing the horses to rear. The wheels speeded up and Wingy, knocked to the street, found her right arm pinned between two spokes of a wagon wheel.

It was a miracle that her arm was not ripped off—but from this time on her arm was frozen into a ludicrous V-shape. It stuck out from the shoulder, extending the horizontal shoulder line; then the lower arm pointed in at her waist, completing the V. The V could swing back and forth and she could use her fingers somewhat, but she could not unfold her arm. When she ran, her arm would flap, like the wing of a flying bird.

So from this time on we began to call her "Wingy." Her real name was Mary.

She was lonely. We boys in the gang, cruel as children can be, scorned her company.

Many people would have been crushed by such a misfortune, but not Mary. She continued to be a tomboy, to wear her shapeless tomboy clothes. She could no longer swim in the East River with her crippled arm, so she began to take long walks along the waterfront.

Many people would have retreated into a shell, confining themselves to their dark, silent rooms, cursing their fate, hating the world, hating themselves.

Not Wingy! She found new life—at the waterfront.

A girl in a boy's and man's world, often an object of ridicule because of her deformed arm, she refused to deny her worth as a human being. *She did not give up on herself*.

It was early summer when Wingy discovered the world of the waterfront; the ships sailing in to port to be unloaded; the husky longshoremen slashing their hooks into the bales of merchandise from foreign lands; hard-working men cursing in the sun.

She liked to watch and soon made friends with one of the longshoremen, an artist with the hook, a man of sweat and profanity. He was surprised when she said she was a girl—she dressed like a very sloppy boy.

But he accepted her interest; so did the other men. They put her to work as hauler and runner, carrying water buckets, fetching equipment. Her right arm would flap back and forth while her left arm hauled and carried, hauled and carried.

Soon she was a fixture, running up and down this East River pier, hauling and fetching with her one good arm. She earned food for lunch, and pay.

She did what she had to do, and everyone respected her.

In late October, Indian summer came; the days were hot. We went to the East River, our gang of fellows, and jumped around on the sand barges. Suddenly one of the boys, Red, was screaming for help.

We tried to help Red, but he was wedged between the side of the barge and the edge of the pier. His foot was caught and he was terrified. So were we; a gust of wind could blow the barge into the pier and Red, sandwiched in between, could be crushed—even killed.

We could do nothing. He was in such a position that only one of us could reach him at a time; no *one* of us was strong enough to pull him free.

So someone ran for help.

Help came. It was Wingy, paddling the air with her right arm as she ran, a scarecrow blowing in the wind.

We told her to leave, but she kneeled on the pier, reached her left arm out to Red—and pulled him free.

We were shocked; we couldn't believe our eyes.

Working with the longshoremen, Wingy's left arm had grown strong. She had saved Red.

Soon we elected her president of our gang of boys—this crippled, unwanted little girl. Finally, we respected her too.

She was not always a tomboy, this stouthearted little Mary.

Later on surgery restored her right arm to normalcy. Then

she resigned as president of our boys' gang. More of a girl, then a young woman, she married and began to have children.

This is not unusual; most tomboys do settle into their natural role as they develop.

What is unusual is that Wingy, in refusing to let her crippled arm force her to retire from life, gained an inner strength—a resoluteness—which had never been so much hers before.

I remember her not so much for the heroic rescue of Red, but because she would not withdraw from life. She was a person, at an early age, who would not quit when the situation became painful.

As long as she lives, I feel sure that Wingy will always remain young and vital. She will always accept herself, as herself, with no fantasy, no narcissism. She will meet life as best she can.

The Symbol of Aliveness

Wingy will always remain in my mind as a symbol of aliveness for a person like her, who will not give up on herself even in adversity, will always be alive. A person with her unswerving belief in herself, ignoring the opinions of others, will never retire from life into a self-imposed dungeon of darkness.

This is in sharp contrast to others I have known—in my practice, as acquaintances and friends, or people who came to see me after reading my books—who found life difficult to endure because they disliked themselves with such a perverse passion.

One such was the adolescent girl, clumsy with her hands and always conscious of her clumsiness, who had overheard her parents talking about her "clumsy" piano playing when she was a little girl. Dedicating her life to the image of herself as "clumsy," this girl not only played the piano poorly but was poor in all areas involving manual dexterity, such as sewing. Her self-criticism extended to other aspects of herself until her mind in late adolescence was a beehive of stinging self-blame. Fear was her dominant emotion until

I explained to her that she couldn't be held responsible for the opinions of others. She got the message. Now as an adult, she plays piano well. She cooks well. She sews well.

Or the adolescent boy, son of a doctor I knew, who had joined a rowdy gang and carried a knife in his pocket, a troublemaker at school with bad grades in almost all his classes. At fifteen resentment was his dominant emotion, and in his eyes you could feel his lack of trust in people until I showed him he could be a successful person and rise above resentment.

Or the many boys and girls, men and women I had known in my lifetime as a plastic surgeon who—given a new face, with the opportunity to expand on this newness and feel enthusiasm for the change and the possibilities—could feel no joy because they had really given up on themselves before the operation.

So much suffering in people; so much suffering that people impose on themselves. I have seen it for months and years—and for decades.

It is my happiness that I was able to help some of these people to feel better about themselves. It is my fulfillment that I was able to make some of them see that their truth about themselves was not real—or that it was only a partial truth.

Some of them regained their spark—and began to smile at life. From their dark retirement within their minds, they reached outward toward the world—a world which they found, even with its unceasing problems, was a far better place to live in.

Like Wingy, some of them fought their way through their problems and their handicaps—physical and emotional—to function happily in a world in which this is not always easy.

Some learned to smile.

Some learned to feel respect for themselves.

Some found life within themselves.

Aliveness at Any Age

If it is aliveness that we seek so ardently, we can find it at any chronological stage in our lives. When we think of aliveness, we think of a freshness and vigor, a spring to the step and a ring to the laugh. We think of driving curiosity, of eager creativity.

The American poet Helen Hunt Jackson once wrote that "whom the gods love, live young forever."

I don't know who the "gods" love, but I do know that if you have a gentle respect for yourself, a belief in your fundamental goodness, you will feel alive and "young" as long as you live. You will not dedicate your years to inertia and complaint, to the emptying out of your woes into the nearest ears (which you hope will be sympathetic). No, the bubble will not have burst; the fires will still burn brightly within you; your creative urge will be a compelling force.

Vitality, creative vitality in all your years; each day full of goals, aflame with earnest endeavor. No matter what your age, rich or poor, this must be one of your most cherished aims.

When does your preparation start? It starts *right* now.

If you are sixteen or forty-six or sixty-six, it starts right *now*.

You begin with a basic process of self-education; it is a fairly simple process, yet we all seem to overlook it in the smothering clamor of miscellaneous, often irrelevant, data that clutter up our minds in this hustle-bustle world of ours.

In this self-educative process you need master the terminology of no dictionary. You don't have to hold college degrees or to understand the Theory of Relativity.

You must simply come to grips with yourself.

You must assert the power and integrity of your self-image.

You must establish the authentic dignity of your self-image on a realistic base as a foundation for full living at your present age—now.

Life is not a picnic; sometimes there is no food at all, and ants and mosquitoes to boot. You must survive your failures and disappointments, charge back off the floor and keep punching. There are no handouts; you can expect only what you give yourself. You can only count on the spark and fire and friendliness which you, the thinker, give you, the acting person in life.

Suppose you lose your job or your business venture is failing. You feel depressed; who wouldn't? You feel frustrated, perhaps nervous or angry. For two or three days you may be hard to get along with; fair-weather friends will avoid you and dogs will bark. But how are you thinking now that all this is in the past? Are you bogged down in a swamp of gloom, blaming yourself for your mistakes, hating those whose actions hurt you? Is your mind a staccato messenger of criticism, piercing you with reminders of what you might have done and with what you might have been? Do you see yourself over and over, blundering, and hate what you see so much that you end up losing sight of yourself entirely, blotting out the self-image that is your best friend in life?

Or do you see yourself kindly? Do you see yourself making your mistakes, yet forgive yourself and tell yourself that you are only human? Do you then resolve to avoid this type of mistake, if possible, yet with a determination to accept yourself if you err again? Do you then see yourself in your good moments, making wise choices, carrying out intelligent actions, achieving what you wanted to achieve? Do you carry this image of yourself back into your mind, this image of yourself accomplishing your goals, this image of yourself as the kind of person you can be?

If you can rebound from failure—any failure—in this accepting, nonjudgmental, positive way, your self-image once more restored, on your side, you will feel vitality all the years of your life. Your problems will not terrify you when you think of them; instead you will feel hope because the pattern of your thinking is hopeful.

Children Three-to-Six
on the Way to Creative Lives

You cannot start too early to build creative habits of living.

At the Forsyth School in St. Louis, under the directorship of Mrs. Mary Dunbar, children of three to six unknowingly are absorbing concepts, based on my book *Psycho-Cybernetics,* which some day will lead to positive adult living. The several hundred children in this school learn goal-mindedness, proper use of the imagination, acceptance of mistakes, compassion for their fellows, and other basic principles associated with the success mechanism, psycho-cybernetics, and self-image psychology.

They learn to live in harmony with each other.

The principal told me how a group of six-year-olds constructed a city in a huge sandbox; then a little toddler of three demolished it during lunch hour. The six-year-old boys conferred, then explained to the principal that the little tyke didn't know what he was doing.

"We can build it over again," one said, "and it will be even better."

I visited the school recently and was most impressed with the positive habits these small children were forming.

During an exercise period, the small boys crawled hand over hand on bars. One couldn't keep up with the others.

He was instructed to sit in a chair and think in his mind how he looked when he failed, how the others looked when they succeeded.

The next day, I was told, he mastered the bars.

The only teacher-imposed discipline is a "thinking chair." A child who hurts another must sit in it and think of who he is and what he did.

While I was there, a little fellow was squirming in the chair when the child he had hurt felt compassion for him and brought him a book so that he could spend his time pleasantly.

A four-year-old whipped by, tricycle wheels flashing, chortling, *"I've got go-power!"*

At one point a group of six-year-olds was studying "Ill" words.

"K-i-l-l," said one.

"We don't use that word," corrected another. "Make that s-k-i-l-l."

"I have a 'gold' in my computer," said one little girl. She meant "goal."

And she did have a goal.

They all did.

At three to six, in this school for the very young, these children were taking dead aim on habits that would lead them successfully through childhood, adolescence, young maturity, and middle age, into years of productive retirement-age living—training for creative lives, today.

No, you cannot start too early.

Exercise 3

If your self-image is weak, crowds probably disturb you.

You are walking along the street, let us say. It is a beautiful day; the sky is blue and the sun is shining. You enjoy walking, it is fun; the trouble is that there are too many people. Before you know it, your little walk feels tiresome; "too many people," you tell yourself. "I feel like an ant in an ant colony."

Worries and resentments take over; there is no joy left in your walking. It is just another of the agonies in your life. All you can think of, one of the crowd, is how insignificant you are.

This is an improper use of your imagination—of your self-image-ination. You are downgrading yourself, without realizing it.

Other people live with crowds in this crowded world; some don't mind them, some even like them. You need not lose your sense of self just because you are surrounded by other selves.

These ideas will help you; try them next time you're in a crowd or in some similar situation:

1. See in your mind a past success of yours, even a partial success. Picture the situation in your mind; see it in techni-

color if you can, feel it. You were pleased with yourself; recapture this feeling of self-satisfaction and bring it into focus. Make this success part of your self-image; forget your failures and concentrate on this success. Do not be grandiose or conceited; these are only inferiority feelings in reverse. Just keep this pleasant image alive in your mind, and feel good about yourself.

2. Visualize another happy moment in your life and keep seeing it. Instead of envying some person in the crowd who looks self-satisfied, see this other image of yourself which helps you feel successful. Stay with it, and don't let yourself feel guilty because you're indulging yourself. If you don't think of yourself first, no one else will. You can be sure of that.

3. As you're walking along, enjoying the vibrant feel of movement, building your confidence with the memory of your real successes, plan your next goal for the day. Think of something you can move toward, something you want to do, and figure out how you're going to move toward it. Plan your strategy, foresee the realistic obstacles—and anticipate the possible rationalizations you may use to block yourself. Is this goal realistic for you now? If not, put it off until its realization is within your reach. But if you want to do it, if you're ready to do it, don't put it off till "tomorrow," which may never come.

Make this exercise—and all the exercises in this book —daily goals. They will help you to live more creatively —now.

Preparing for Growth and Fun

It is important to understand this principle: that, just as you spend your teen years preparing for your lifework, you should spend your whole life living creatively and preparing for future years of dynamic living.

You prepare when you build a self-image which will sustain you during these years and which will allow you years of growth and fun.

You cannot start too young—or too old.

For anyone reading this book who understands that the

fight for happiness is a battle of thoughts and images in your mind, the time to start is now.

Not tomorrow.

Now .

You owe it to yourself.

In the pages of this book, you will find many exercises which are designed to help you to help yourself. Work on them.

Now.

When you try, you are there!

One little girl of six at the Forsyth School told her mother: "Try, try again, that's what we learn at Forsyth School, Mommy . . . If at first you don't conceive . . . try, try again!"

• 5 •

Years of Success for You

"THIS BOOK," you may say, "will not help me because my health is poor. Sugarcoated words will not help."

My words are not sugarcoated; they represent the truth as I see it.

"I've always had bad luck," you may say. "Why should my luck change?"

No one gets all bad breaks; what are you doing to help yourself?

"I've got no money in the bank and I owe everybody I know. What's the use?"

Everyone has troubles, friend. I'm writing for people in this world, not for angels in paradise.

Some of the most creative people in our national history fought their way past severe handicaps.

Benjamin Franklin left school at ten to assist his father, and was apprenticed to his half brother at twelve.

Andrew Jackson, our seventh President, was an orphan

at fourteen when his mother died. Jackson educated himself, reading law books in his spare time.

Ulysses S. Grant, our eighteenth President, was a failure in everyone's eyes when the Civil War broke out; labeled an erratic alcoholic, Grant was a brilliant tactician who played a big part in the North's winning of the Civil War.

It is axiomatic that reality is not always what we'd like it to be. We live with problems every day; we struggle and do the best we can, go to sleep and struggle some more. Sometimes we succeed, sometimes we fail; no one succeeds all the time. Few people have realistic problems so severe as to cripple their application of an active philosophy and to blunt their development of a healthy self-image.

Most people magnify their complaints, build them out of proportion, worry about a minor physical symptom or a little bad fortune—and do their best to worry other people too. Exaggerated anxiety runs rampant among people today.

Worry, worry, worry, but where will it get you?

You, reading this book, recharge your batteries with the ideas that you'll find. Within you is a success mechanism which will work for you if you put into motion attitudes which are oriented toward your well-being.

Do not allow unessential complaints to undermine your success instincts. Do not let them force you into a premature withdrawal from life.

Forget your minor problems. Concentrate on your assets. Move toward life with the best that is in you.

Sympathy Will Get You Nowhere

Do you feel sorry for yourself? Do you enjoy reciting your endless complaints to people—anyone will do, really —so they can cluck their tongues and shake their heads dolefully? Maybe some people will even tell you how brave you are to endure such suffering.

This sympathy, plus five cents, will no longer buy you a good cup of coffee. It will give your soul no basic nourishment, only an imitation of food for your sustenance.

Even the other person's expression of compassion may be faked. When you walk past him, he may say to himself,

"Poor soul, he's going to worry himself to death (if he doesn't worry me to death first)."

Of course others may be concerned.

The English poet Shelley once wrote that "My heart was pierced with sympathy for woe which could not be my own."

This is a compassionate feeling and I applaud it, as I generally would applaud the compassionate sentiments of any person human enough to feel for another human in distress. Nevertheless, from the point of view of the sufferer, the receiving of sympathy cannot make up for the pain he endures.

Martyrdom is never worthwhile—even if others shed tears for you and line your path with roses.

The real life is one composed of vibrant days, in which a person goes out to find the joys in the world, actively, to the full extent of his physical powers, instead of curling up by himself in a ball of frustrated "nondoingness," hating his misery and his womblike shell of indifference.

You must feel, first, that you have the right to be happy. You must sing in your heart that you are one of God's creatures, born to live and laugh and love. You must tell yourself that you owe life something, and that life owes you something. Forget your past blunders; renounce your guilts; cancel out your mistakes. Think of yourself at your best, doing good for yourself and others, and feel that you deserve satisfactions.

Then you will not look to your minor complaints to reinforce a sense of misery which you feel you really merit.

"I Just Wanted To Help"

Recently I went to Lake Orion, near Detroit, Michigan, to talk to a group of priests who have succumbed to alcoholism. They come from all over the world and are treated for four months and return to their flocks cured. During the stage of sobriety, they use my book *Psycho-Cybernetics* as a bridge to walk back to themselves, and they do.

After lecturing, I went to sleep for a few hours. I was awakened at 1:45 A.M. Lake Orion is about forty-five miles from Detroit, and I had to catch the 4:35 plane back to New York so that I could operate on a child who had been seriously injured in an automobile accident.

The night man, after waking me, took me to the main house of the priests' sanitarium and made me scrambled eggs and coffee.

This simple action touched me for it was not his job, and I had not asked him to make a meal for me.

He stood there, bushy hair, rosy cheeks, and asked me if the eggs were okay.

"Fine," I said, and thanked him for putting himself out for me at 2:00 A.M.

"I just wanted to help," he said and gave me a shy, friendly smile.

After some small talk, he told me about himself. He had a bad heart. Under his shirt he wore a pacemaker, an electrical instrument attached to the chest wall. This instrument helped him keep his heart beating normally, enabled him to live and work as night man at the sanitarium.

"Another cup of coffee?" he asked.

I nodded.

"I like to help," he said. "I really do. Since I had my heart trouble, especially, I live a good life. I like to help people, and I take other people's help. I've got no complaints."

On the plane from Detroit to New York, I thought about this man who lived a simple life and enjoyed it. I said to myself, "If a man who can't live without an electrical instrument will not give in, we can all learn the lesson that, despite our problems, we can stand up to the stresses of the day and refuse to withdraw from our strength, activating our success mechanisms, every day, living each day to the full."

Hope for You

"While there's life, there's hope," is a saying of merit—if you feel that you deserve the good things in life, if your concept of yourself will support the idea of happiness.

Unfortunately, too many people shortchange themselves; they would never do this with money, yet they do it with thoughts. Some individuals rob themselves of everything. They worry about every minor problem.

That's why the story of this man—on-the-job and happy despite a bad heart—should be an inspiring one to people whose courage has vanished under the onslaught of fears.

The strength of his self-image—plus his pacemaker for his heart—keep him living a good life. You do not need a pacemaker for your heart? Then let your self-image be your pacemaker. Let your pleasant image of yourself give you what you need to go toward the world in the confident, aggressive, giving spirit that leads to patterns of exciting experiences.

This is your hope.

When I was younger, the intelligence quotient (IQ) was supposed to be very significant. A person would take some "intelligence" tests and receive a score. If he answered most of the questions correctly, he was labeled as a "genius" or as gifted; if he was slow or clumsy in answering the questions, he was considered subnormal or perhaps an absolute dunce.

A youngster who scored high on these IQ tests was thought of, often, as earmarked for success, while one who scored low was considered stupid—after the breadlines, then what?

I was always skeptical of the value of his IQ evaluation. My doubts have been confirmed. For years I have seen high-IQ people who have ruined their lives, low-IQ people who have lived productively.

Your self-image is so much more basic to your happiness; surely you must realize this. To me it seems obvious. If you are not only as intelligent as Albert Einstein, but also as charming as Fred Astaire and as good a golfer as Jack Nicklaus or Gary Player, you will still not enjoy life if you judge yourself critically, if you look for reasons to degrade yourself. If your self-image is weak, your positive qualities do not matter—they're irrelevant; you will find ways to torture yourself. Nothing you do will be good enough.

Therefore, when you start a day, looking for something hopeful to get you off on the right foot, don't ask, "How's my IQ today?" Instead, ask yourself, "How's my self-image? How's my S-I?" Your IQ is not important. It depends on the opinion of others. Your S-I *is* important. It depends on the opinion of yourself. Without a proper opinion of yourself, you can't function creatively.

If your S-I is all right, you can forget about your IQ and you will enjoy your day. When you walk in the street and the sun is shining, you might even find yourself whistling a tune that you love.

Your Guide to Success

Our lives are so complicated—tangled up as they are in bank accounts, insurance policies, income taxes, furniture, relatives, telephone numbers, and all kinds of miscellaneous data about automobile mileage and meteorological reports—that we often lose sight of fundamental truths.

One fundamental truth is that we all have within us instincts for successful survival in the world.

Obstacles may come, troubles may come—who knows, as Professor Higgins complained in *My Fair Lady*, but that your relatives may invade you in force—but you have within you, all of you, those success instincts which I call your success mechanism.

The fight to free these instincts, to harness them to the struggle for life, is largely an internal one. You must argue it out with yourself. You must decide whether you are determined to live the good life; you must convince yourself that the good things are your right.

This is not always easy because many of you have been indoctrinated with the belief that you were born to suffer. This is a belief that you must root out with as much urgency as you would feel if you had unwitttingly swallowed a bottle of poison.

You must remind yourself that you can feel successful and happy—and *you* must set the standards which constitute your success. It must be a success *in your image,* or it is a failure.

An interesting story comes to mind. I told this story a few years ago while lecturing at Town Hall in New York.

When Franklin D. Roosevelt was President, I performed an operation on a friend of his wife's. Mrs. Roosevelt invited me to the White House in Washington; I was to spend the night in the Yellow Room, near the room where someone told me Abraham Lincoln had slept.

I was flattered. No, I was overwhelmed. I didn't sleep at all that night. Instead, I sat up writing my mother, my friends—even my enemies—on White House stationery.

As a kid I had played in the streets of a tough New York neighborhood, the Lower East Side.

"Max," I said to myself, "you have arrived."

In the morning I went downstairs to breakfast where Mrs. Eleanor Roosevelt was hostess. She was a lovely lady; there was extraordinary charm in her eyes. I accepted scrambled eggs on my plate and was then led to a tray piled high with kippers. I eat almost everything, but I had always detested kippers. I looked at the kippers with horror.

Mrs. Roosevelt smiled at me. "Frank loves kippers," she said, referring to the President.

I considered. "Who am I?" I thought, "to refuse these kippers? Surely what's good enough for the President is good enough for me?"

So I helped myself to kippers, ate them with the eggs—and that afternoon I was sick. In the evening I was still nauseous.

What is the meaning of this story?

Simple.

I lost sight of my image of myself.

I did not want the kippers and did not have to eat them. In trying to imitate the President, out of respect, I betrayed my self-image. It was a minor betrayal; its ill-effects were superficial and did not last too long.

Still, it points to one of the most common pitfalls on the road to success.

A success in other people's eyes, which you do not initiate as a consummation of your desires, in your image, is not a success.

It is a failure.

Deeply imbedded in the American culture today, with the helpless passivity of a six-week-old baby clinging to its mother, is a complex which someone called "keeping up with the Joneses." The basic idea of this complex is that if your neighbor or your friend has a new car, you must have one too, if he has a new house, you must buy one too—and where this silly competition ends, I don't know.

What I do know is that this form of "success" is failure; it takes away from a person's concept of the integrity of his self. He renounces the status of his own image, as I did when I imitated President Roosevelt, and involves himself in a meaningless competition which does not satisfy his soul.

Remember this: *Your surest guide to success is your acceptance of yourself, living the best you can.*

A poor man can be more successful than a king if his self-image is stronger.

If you would read these words cynically, thinking to yourself, "He doesn't really believe that," recall to your mind the great statesmen, millionaires, movie actors, public figures who have committed suicide or drowned themselves in other forms of misery because they could not come to terms with themselves.

Because a poor man can be more successful than a king.

You, rich or poor, young or old, can feel successful if you understand the power of your thoughts and images and will, in your mind, a sense of success.

Then you will be ready to go toward your goals and live each day fully.

Bring Back Your Strength

When I was a boy, living in an apartment house on the Lower East Side, we had a piano in the living room. Often my father, mother, sister, and I would cluster around the piano and sing folk songs. "My Bonnie Lies Over the Ocean" was one song which we would sing.

Do you remember the words of this old favorite, so popular fifty years ago when families felt comfort in banding together and sharing the good spirit of group singing? It goes like this:

> *My bonnie lies over the ocean,*
> *My bonnie lies over the sea,*
> *My bonnie lies over the ocean,*
> *Oh, bring back my bonnie to me.*

Bring back, bring back,
Oh, bring back my bonnie to me, to me,
Bring back, bring back,
Oh, bring back my bonnie to me.

The words are plaintive, reflecting the longing of one person
for a loved one. The repetition of the same words "bring
back" emphasizes the desperation of this longing, the urgency
of the need. Separation from a loved one—how sad this is!
What is sadder in life than the feeling of being separated
from people one loves? If one tries to feel the words of a
song such as this, tries really to *feel,* without attempt at con-
cealment, melancholy must result and tears may flow to
soothe the hurt.

Yet there is a separation even more agonizing, infinitely
more painful. This is the separation of a person from his
self-image and from the success mechanism within him which
flows from a healthy self-image.

Much as one may feel the absence of people one loves,
there is nothing to compare—in terms of loneliness—with
one's alienation from his own inner source of comfort.

Too many people spend their lives mourning the death
of a loved one, the disappearance of a joy, the absence of a
state of pleasure—when what they *must* "bring back" is
their ability to see themselves in their best moments, a friend
to themselves no matter what the troubles they may have to
endure in the world.

"Bring back" your successful image of yourself; "bring
back" your spirit of participation in life.

That is your "bonnie."

When you are overcome by some negative feeling that
takes you away from your true self, take a moment off, look
in the mirror as a little bonus exercise, and sing this song,
substituting the words "my image" for "my bonnie."

My image lies over the ocean,
My image lies over the sea,
My image lies over the ocean,
Oh, bring back my image to me.

Bring back, bring back,
Oh, bring back my image to me, to me,
Bring back, bring back,
Oh, bring back my image to me.

The Threads of Love

Years ago, traveling in Nicaragua where I had some operations scheduled, I went to the home of a wealthy, aristocratic young couple.

Urgently they took me to the crib. Almost in desperation, they pointed to the girl baby in the crib, four months old. They pointed to her lip, which was an abomination to them.

The child had been born with a harelip—a cleft in her upper lip.

"Could I do anything?" they asked.

I nodded my head.

Hope replaced tension in their eyes.

Driving me away, a friend filled me in on the story. Before the birth of the baby, they had been regarded as an ideal couple. On both sides, their families were wealthy coffee people. Not only were they rich, and descendants of families long influential in Nicaragua, but they were both handsome and loved each other.

Then came the baby—with the harelip.

Suspicions were immediate. The girl's father accused the boy's family of bad blood. The boy's mother insulted the girl's heredity.

Hatred now instead of harmony. Like the families of Romeo and Juliet, the families now hated the idea of the marriage. One hundred years before these families had been feuding, and the grandparents, remembering the old grudge battle, reactivated the bitterness.

Two old men on opposing sides fought a ridiculous duel with swords; both, unwounded, left the field of battle muttering curses. The women would no longer talk to each other. The young married couple were trying to keep their love alive, but the strain was showing. People said nothing could be done to heal the breach.

In the hospital operating room I felt a strong sense of the theatrical. I felt I was doing more than surgery. I felt that I was weaving the threads of love in bringing the two edges of the baby's lips together . . . in bringing the families together.

The child was put under anesthesia. As she lay relaxed on the table, I pared the edges of the cleft. The bleeding was easily controlled. First, the central area of muscle of the lip hidden by skin above and mucous membrane inside the mouth was separated from the skin outside and from the mucous membrane inside. This central muscular layer I brought together with a few firm catgut stitches, to be absorbed when healing was complete. Then I stitched the edges of the mucous membrane on the inside of the mouth with fine silk threads; I also stitched the skin externally. Dressings covered the lip to prevent pulling of the stitches.

The tiny patient was returned to her room and came out of the anesthetic shortly. Two days later she was discharged from the hospital. I changed the dressings daily. On the eighth day I removed the fine silk stitches painlessly, and after two weeks I removed the dressings for good.

I stood aside after removing the final dressing, and the two families pressed around the crib to look at the baby's lip. A cry of joy went up; the lip was fine.

A grandfather squeezed the baby's toe fiercely. He explained that he did this to make the baby cry "like a normal child."

Harmony came back into the lives of the young married couple, their families patched up their differences, and life went on in Nicaragua.

Exercise 4

It made me feel happy, of course, to help these people, but that is not my reason for telling this story. My point is that, though these people had acted wisely in trying to correct an imperfection, at the same time they were terribly foolish in magnifying the importance of the defect.

These ideas will help you:

1. When you have an "emotional harelip" (hurt feelings, guilt, resentment), a negative feeling that creates a gap between you and your true self, between you and others, be your own plastic surgeon. Without a knife, but with compassion for yourself, repair the gap between you and your true self-image, between you and others. Close the gap with threads of love. Reread this modern-day version of Romeo and Juliet, and benefit from it by resolving not to imitate the foolishness of these feuding families.

2. If you are unable to correct this defect—and we all have one form of "emotional harelip" or another—learn to live with it. Stop blaming yourself; be a good friend instead. If you were perfect, you would be so different from the rest of us that no one would talk to you.

3. Once you feel a little better about your "harelips," think about your good features. Are you patient? Are you tactful? Are you considerate of others? Are you aggressive when aggressiveness is appropriate? Are you a good friend in a crisis? Are you loyal? Are you an efficient worker? Be pleased about yourself; stop thinking about your minuses, and concentrate on your pluses.

4. See yourself in a successful moment; see it in your mind. See it and feel it. Once again, picture yourself in a definite situation in which you are happy about yourself, and flash this picture over and over in your mind. You have done this in other exercises already; do it again because it is so important. Regain the feel of your success—over and over and over.

Your Hope for a Creative Life

". . . In health or in sickness, till death us do part." These are familiar words, taken from the marriage vow.

The words symbolize union, a union of two people in a serious undertaking which ideally would bring them prosperity and happiness.

So it must be with you and your active life force, which should never be buried in a coffin called "no money" or "bad luck" or whatever. It should also never be stuffed into a coffin labeled "minor physical complaints."

So it must be with you and your image of yourself, which must be your ally in times of adversity. If you support yourself in good times and desert yourself when things go wrong, you are no friend to yourself.

Your quest for the good things should not be abandoned when things go wrong. It should, if anything, be accelerated. If you abandon this quest, you are a traitor to yourself.

Do you revile Benedict Arnold for his renunciation of country in a critical time? Why, then, do you not similarly revile yourself if you undermine your own strivings needlessly?

During the Civil War, Abraham Lincoln once said, "If there is a worse place than Hell, I am in it."

But Lincoln stayed with it, one of our most creative Presidents, until he had saved the Union.

Just as a person must come well-born into this world, so he must live in a creative, meaningful way, weaving artistry into the pattern of his years. He must worship the life force within him and bequeath to himself the understanding that to squander it is an act of treachery to himself.

If you feel that you are a worthwhile person, and if you can free yourself from your preoccupation with unimportant complaints, you will enjoy your days infinitely more.

Years of creative living.

Experience-rich, hour-full, perfection-less, grudge-proof years, in which your experimenting having honed your creative forces razor-sharp, you will be equipped to live sensibly.

It could be that your greatest successes await you.

Success Goals
for Creative Living

"WHAT KIND OF a book on creative living is this?" you might wonder. "No information on money management, no data on groups to join, nothing on recreational activities that could be helpful. Aren't these worthwhile, also?"

Certainly they are. For in the final analysis, while it is your support of yourself that will bring you delight or heartbreak, these external factors play a definite part in your environment and in your adjustment to this environment.

You can find information on many subjects pertinent to creative living in many books, and your librarian can guide you to some of them. I do not include these materials because they are available in these other books and because the writers of these books know much more about these factors than I do.

The value of this book, however, and the reason that I consider it to be possibly the most valuable book that I have ever written, is that it focuses on the two major pitfalls of people: (1) withdrawal from life and (2) reliance upon factors outside of one's concept of one's own worth.

For this is the truth: *It is the health of your self-image that will allow you to enjoy life with a minimum of fear and worry.*

People who truly enjoy life have a sense of continuity. Their goals flow into goals and merge; their days flow into days and meet. They feel pride in the worth of their lives; they rise above fear.

Having goals is creative, useful concentration. You must have goals; each day you must have something to aim at. Living each day fully, overcoming worry and resentment, is a goal in itself.

When you wake up in the morning and throw off the sheets, you must get into the habit of rooting the pre-breakfast worries out of your mind and, instead, replacing them with aims that will make your day exciting. This must be automatic, as automatic as washing your face, combing your hair, shaving off your beard, or applying lipstick.

Years of days with goals—goals that are *your* goals. Not goals that other people have foisted upon you—*your* goals.

Your Goals Are Your Own

These must be your goals, or your efforts will do you no good. As a rational human being, you must crystallize your thinking, eliminate the irrelevancies, get to the heart of *you,* to see what it is that you want to achieve.

Don't let conventional thinking take away from your determination in setting *your* goals. If it is satisfying for you to build a table, that is a worthy goal—even if it impresses no one but yourself. If it is boring for you to write a five hundred-page book, thoroughly researched and documented, this is not a worthy goal because you do not grow in the process—no matter that other people praise you.

No goal is too insignificant if it contributes to your sense of achievement. It cannot be small; only *you* can make it small.

The English poet Robert Browning once wrote:

> That low man seeks a little thing to do,
> Sees it and does it:
> This high man, with a great thing to pursue,
> Dies ere he knows it.
>
> That low man goes on adding one to one,
> His hundred's soon hit:
> This high man, aiming at a million,
> Misses an unit.
> —*A Grammarians Funeral*

Add "one to one" and hit your "hundred"; maybe you'll reach the age of one hundred and be "hitting your thousands."

In the process of "hitting" goals, you will also miss some —assuming that you are human. These failures should not inhibit you, should not stop you from tackling new projects optimistically. A child learns through trial-and-error; so does an adult. Constructive criticism can be helpful, but self-blame in the form of guilt is only destructive.

The Roman poet-satirist Horace, whose wisdom has survived two thousand years, once wrote: "Nor will the arrow always strike the mark at which it was aimed."

True. Sometimes you will miss the bull's-eye completely. Some days you may mumble to yourself that there was really no point in getting out of bed; the whole day was a mistake.

But even then, your next day is a lifetime—a lifetime with an exciting goal, or goals. You will bury the past day, will think about it no more. For each day is a whole. And this day dawning, this will be rewarding!

The English novelist George Eliot (her real name was Mary Ann Evans) once wrote that "What makes life dreary is the want of motive."

But this is your responsibility to yourself; you must give yourself motive. You must build the road to your enrichment; you must set the cement. Then you must start the motor and travel down the road you have created.

The Fire within You

A fire of enthusiasm burns within you; only *you* can put it out. You can put out this inner fire if you are too lazy, or too full of self-defeat to put fuel on the fire. Any fire will die if there is no fuel.

But you will keep the fire alive. Once you have your goals, you will tackle them with intensity. Your life instinct will be at its height.

For it is this sense of intense interest in what they are doing that propels people to success.

The late Edward R. Murrow's success as a broadcaster was based largely on his deep interest in what he was discussing. In watching Murrow on TV, you could not escape his emotional and intellectual involvement in his subject, whether it was political freedom, civil rights, poverty, individual personalities, or an event in a world where startling things happen.

The great success of an actor like James Cagney or an actress like Bette Davis stems from the intensity they project; they light up the screen with their electric personalities.

The example of Thomas Edison is a classic one; here was a man with such a consuming interest in the goals which he set for himself.

People know Edison mostly as the inventor of the incandescent electric lamp. Few realize the full scope of his incredible achievements.

Among Edison's monumental inventions are the phonograph, the electric locomotive, the microphone, a method for constructing concrete buildings, the electric pen, a device for producing sheet metal, the cinematograph, a district telegraph signal box, a contribution to the Bell telephone, starting and current-supplying systems for automobiles. These are just a *few* of this intensely creative man's inventions; the entire list leaves one in a state of disbelief.

The final utilization of his ideas resulted in the modern electronic tube. This tube, in its many forms, is the basis for radio broadcasting, long distance telephoning, the X ray, sound pictures, TV, and a considerable number of other industries, again more than I can list.

In 1928 Congress presented Edison with a Gold Medal and estimated his inventive contributions to humanity at $15,599,000,000. What they would be worth today is probably too great for any human being to grasp.

And Thomas Edison's entire formal education consisted of three months in public school, where his teacher described him as a young boy who daydreamed too much and would never succeed in life.

What was Edison's great secret?

One was his ability to set goals and the enthusiasm with which he pursued them. Once he set a goal, he would adapt his life to it, and it would *become* his life. Then he would give to and take from life through his goals—until, if I may be permitted a play on words, "the air would sparkle with electricity."

He would read inexhaustibly on his project—book after book. Then he would send out for more books.

He would start work in his laboratory only after his reading had prepared him to undertake his experiments intelligently. Then he worked long hours; often he arrived at his lab before 8:00 A.M. and was not finished until 2 or 3 A.M. the following day. His focus was always sharp and intense so there was no wasted motion. Performing hundreds of experiments, selecting and discarding models, enduring the inevitable failures, he kept driving straight ahead until he reached his goal.

There was great certainty of purpose in Edison, finely honed goal selection. Along with his great imagination and intelligence, this concentration on and enthusiasm for his goals helped make him one of the great inventive minds in the history of mankind.

Another fact about Edison is highly revealing of his strong sense of direction. When he was on vacation, he played just as hard as he did when he worked. He would not dilute his goals of play, either; he would refuse to talk about work when he was vacationing.

Foreign nations honored Edison. France, Great Britain, and Italy joined his own country in conferring titles upon him.

He never ran away from life; he never ran away from setting goals.

Live Each Moment Fully

All right, no foreign nations will honor you and maybe today your wife isn't even talking to you. But you can nevertheless learn a lesson from Thomas Edison: the intensity with which one should pursue goals as an essential ingredient of the life process, as an essential obstacle to any projected withdrawal from life.

Is a skeptical thought beginning to inch its way into your mind? Are you thinking, "This is the great Edison. I am only me?" Will such a fallacious thought keep you from grasping an essential point?

It shouldn't. Because Edison was a man, too. A human

being. Just like you. If you had ever met him, his physical appearance might have seemed ordinary to you. Another human being.

But one who set goals, believed in them, pursued them, lived them. Goals were his life. Goals were his days.

This is what one can learn from him; to set goals, each day, every day, and to feel fire for them. To feel fire, that is to live!

We are all different—we are unless, out of fear, we stifle our individuality. Therefore, we have different goals. But we should have similar feelings for them—call it intensity, fire, drive.

No goal is too small; only one's thinking about the goal is small.

I used to know a man who derived great joy from the ocean. His eyes would light up when he talked about it, about the refreshing feel of plunging into the waves. Every day he would bathe his body and his soul in the ocean waters, no matter what the weather. To him the ocean was wine, it was poetry, it was music.

The way he felt about the ocean, this is the way you should feel about your goals. When you feel such passion for your goals, you feel passion for life. You are alive.

Too often our feelings are dead, and we must pull them back to life. We must experience things; too often worry blocks the way.

Suppose you are eating breakfast and reading the newspaper. You have two goals here, small goals in terms of your entire day, but they are important in themselves; to enjoy the food and to absorb the news of the day so that you can achieve further knowledge of your world.

Are you achieving these goals?

"Of course," you say. "These are such simple goals."

But are they? Do you fully experience the rich tang of your orange juice, the crisp brownness of your toast, the stimulating flavor of your coffee?

Or, are you too worried about the war news to even notice what you're eating?

And your newspaper? Do you fully experience its contents in an intelligent way, grasping the world as it is, news-

and politic-wise, creative-wise and with a sense of historical continuity? Is your reading of your newspaper an experience in living; does it increase your capacity for participation in our complex world?

Or is it merely an exercise in worry? Do you worry about the war news, jump with alarm at what some doctor said about hypertension or cancer, and throw the paper away with hysteria on reading about the latest thermonuclear development? Have you merely reinforced your failure mechanism in your reading?

If the negative side wins out, you have not attained your simple goals. You rise from your chair discontented, your breakfast eaten but untasted. You complain about indigestion, rant about the mess the world is in, and head for your work in a vile temper.

You must learn to live each moment fully; you must learn to heighten your feeling about the little things that make life exciting.

There can be joy in biting into your scrambled eggs and bacon; you must rediscover life feelings like these.

How Not To Think

Perhaps you think this way: "I'm fifty-eight and my husband has passed away, my children don't call me, soon I'll be an old woman, and who needs me. I have aches and pains. What is this talk about creative living? What goals do I have to set?"

Or perhaps you say to yourself: "I'm twenty-eight and I should begin thinking about making something of my life—a guy should do the best he can—but life is a rat race, and they might drop the hydrogen bomb, anyway, so why should I bother?"

These negative ways of thinking are, alas, all too common.

"But they are true," you say. "You cannot deny this."

I do deny it; they are not true.

The woman of fifty-eight may have lacks and problems—this is true—but she has opportunities for living, too. She has friends to cultivate, hobbies to enrich her days, small and large tasks to accomplish, thinking to do about her world and her life.

The man of twenty-eight thinks about danger too much. Obviously this world has dangers, but why choke off life because they exist?

Some people talk as if this were the only age in which there were dangers.

This is nonsense.

Two hundred years ago American people were fighting the perils of the wilderness: wild animals, warring Indians, diseases which no one could cure.

About one hundred years ago, with no nuclear weapons, Americans from North and South were slaughtering each other in hand-to-hand catastrophes.

Fifty years ago World War I was bloodying the soil of Europe—and bloodying the minds of human beings who could not escape from their earth-prisons.

Thirty-five years ago a blanket of economic depression was crushing the aspirations of millions of people; many were temporarily helpless beneath its smothering impact.

Even thirty years ago mankind knew serious diseases, fatal diseases—which today are curable.

The fact is that there have always been dangers; human beings must learn to live with them, to deal with them, to enjoy life in spite of them.

Your years—in spite of possible deprivations and dangers —can be rich years.

If you believe that they can be rich years, you can make them so.

This is the way you should think; moreover, this is truthful thinking.

Changing Your "Luck"

"There's some truth in what you say," you may be thinking, but *I* never get a break."

"We've talked about "bad luck" already, but this is such a common way of thinking that we'll take another quick look at it.

The "bad luck" philosophy will only crush your creative

instincts. What's more, it is not even true. And if you think your "luck" is bad, you can change your "luck."

Commodore Vanderbilt, once proud owner of one rowboat in New York Bay, sixty years later was worth ninety million dollars.

Collis P. Huntington was broke when he came to New York at the age of fifteen—and he ended up a millionaire, too.

At twenty-eight, Leland Stanford was victim of a fire which destroyed his law library and other property. He went west and he, too, became one of our wealthiest citizens.

Not that money is everything—it certainly is not—but it doesn't hurt, and often it is evidence of the intensity with which people plunge toward their goals.

I do not absolutely deny that there is such a thing as luck, but it need not run your life. Everyone gets bad breaks at one time or another; everyone gets depressed. But some people ask for defeat; some people shrug off bad "luck" and go on to successes. If their resolution is strong enough, good breaks will generally come their way once more.

Some people even turn bad breaks into creative opportunities.

The great short story writer O. Henry was an unknown when he was accused of embezzlement. He denied the charges but was sentenced to and served three years in prison.

It was while he was in prison that he began writing the short stories that were to bring him great fame.

The time in prison that O. Henry used so well another person might have spent cursing injustice or worrying what people would think of him or telling himself that he never had any kind of luck.

On TV a few years ago, a man told of how he tried to kill himself but failed, blinding himself. After this sad event, he recovered his sense of direction, earning several college degrees and doing well as an author and lecturer. Another man might have cursed the fact that he hadn't killed himself or that he had crippled himself so severely, might have lived out his life bewailing his luck.

When you find you are telling yourself that you are "unlucky," think of these stories. You must fight off a "bad-luck" way of thinking as if you were dealing with an invasion of hostile forces—for that is precisely what you are dealing with.

The constructive way to change your "luck"—and everyone can—is to turn your back on negative feelings and concentrate on the confidence of past successes. You then use this confidence to move toward your present goals.

You may think, "No one forgets his failures," but you can forget.

The more you concentrate on past successes, the more built-in confidence you will feel when you tackle your goals.

In this way you can change your "luck."

Once again, your mind is the battleground, and it is in your mind that you must win your battles.

Exercise 5

I once traveled to Panama to operate on ten or fifteen people with disfigurements. A seven-year-old-boy especially interested me because his right hand was in his trousers pocket and he would not take it out.

He did not speak English, but I got him to understand that I wanted to see his hand. He had a congenital malformation: his index and middle fingers were stuck together, with skin covering them—a birth deformity known as webbed fingers.

He felt terribly sensitive about this condition, I learned. The children on the street would tease him, and he felt inferior to them.

He loved baseball: the big ambition in his life was to play baseball with the other kids. But he couldn't with his deformed right hand; the hand which shamed him he kept in his trousers pocket so people wouldn't see it.

I operated on him to separate his fingers.

Under general anesthesia I separated part of the skin on the outer surface of the index finger from the region of the nail downward from the underlying tissue toward the middle finger. Then I separated the skin on the under surface of the middle finger from the underlying tissue toward the index finger. I cut the soft tissue underneath to separate the two fingers. I rolled the skin flap from the index finger over the raw surface of the middle finger and stitched it in place with very fine silk threads; then I rolled the skin flap from the middle finger over the raw surface of the index finger and stitched it in place. Thus the two fingers were separated.

A week after the operation, I removed the final dressing.

"Raise your hand," I said in Spanish.

He hesitated.

"Go on."

He raised his right hand.

"Now separate your fingers."

Uncertain, he looked at the hand, raised high above his head. Then slowly, slowly, he moved his fingers. His deformity was gone; he could separate them.

A smile broke over his face as he looked at his fingers.

"V for Victory," he shouted in Spanish, and high over his head, his newly separated fingers formed the letter V.

"V for Victory," he repeated.

Now, what can we do with this story?

Because it is the story of a human being's rise—with the help of wonderful modern techniques—from defeat to "V for Victory." Just like the "V" sign popularized during World War II, the boy's "V for Victory" was a symbol of winning out over a universally destructive force—after years of initial defeat and humiliation.

How about a "V for Victory" for you?

You can flash it each day when you look at yourself in the mirror and think of your good moments of that day or of some other day. Forget your failures, stop beating yourself up; think of your successes and see them in your mind.

See them over and over in your mind when you leave the mirror to sit in a chair or walk in the street or lie down on your bed; then make the "V for Victory" sign in your mind, and give yourself credit for what you've done.

Stop feeling sorry for yourself; even if you've had it tough, so have others. This seven-year-old-boy had known shame since his birth; most people have known inner hurt all their lives.

When life seems hard and the breaks seem to be going

against you, be your own plastic surgeon and try, try to cut the emotional deadwood out of yourself.

Each day work on the exercises in this book, seeing yourself at your best, talking sense to yourself, bolstering your sense of self-esteem. Don't laugh at them because they are mental; see if they won't help you, instead.

See if they won't help you to help yourself so that you can overcome your spiritual handicaps—so that you, externally or symbolically, can throw your hand high over your head in triumph in a "V for Victory" celebration.

"V for Victory"—for you!

Goals and Your Success Mechanism

You are setting goals for your days and your years. You have rejected negative thinking which blocks the setting of these goals, and you are proceeding on course.

You may be a young man in your early twenties or a woman in her late forties. You may be setting goals for the day or for tomorrow or for next week. This doesn't matter. What matters is getting into the habit of setting worthwhile goals and then accomplishing them.

Within you, never forget this, are success instincts, and if you can activate them, you have within you a chain reaction of reaching-out-to-achieve-goals mechanisms. This predisposition of a human being toward the successful achievement of his goals, I called the "success mechanism."

*S*ense of direction, *U*nderstanding, *C*harity, *C*ourage, *E*steem, *S*elf-confidence, *S*elf-acceptance—these are the ingredients of your success mechanism. S-U-C-C-E-S-S is what they spell out; S-U-C-C-E-S-S in the nailing down of the goals which you want for yourself.

(Condensed, in different words, from *Psycho-Cybernetics*, hardcover Prentice-Hall, 1960; paperback, Pocket Books, a division of Simon & Schuster, Inc., 1969.)

1. *Sense of direction.* We've gone over this: you must set goals which make sense to *you;* you must know where you're going. A brand-new, smooth-flowing car is of no use if there is no highway.

2. *Understanding.* Many of our goals will center around other people, and we must understand how they think, what they want, how we interact with them. We must be able to communicate with them and to understand the communication they send out to us—no matter how subtle or devious, because of their fears.

3. *Charity.* Understanding other people is fine—but without compassion (or charity) one's reaction is immature and will arouse antagonism in others. For if one understands and blames what one understands, how will this contribute to a caliber of interpersonal relating that leads to harmony and the achievement of goals? Compassionate attitudes toward other people—and, most important, toward oneself—are necessary because, in understanding people, one becomes conscious of the many frailties which are basic to human nature.

4. *Courage.* Setting goals purposefully, understanding and relating well to people—you're on your way to successes. But you must have the courage to *do,* the courage to take a plunge off the diving board, or your success mechanism is incomplete. Because there are no sure things in life and, no matter how well laid your plans, you can never foresee the consequences with certainty. When you have the courage to take action, then your goals in life are more than passing fancies; then they mean something to you in your world.

5. *Esteem.* You must appreciate your own worth as a human being—and that of others. Unless you feel esteem for yourself, your goals are of little value, and even if you achieve them, the victory will be hollow. At the heart of your being must be your feeling that there is good in yourself; if you don't feel this, your successes may impress others, but you will know better. They will be superficial, phony successes. You must learn to see yourself as a child of God, as a creation of His. You must see others, also, as children of God, as purposeful, as valuable.

6. *Self-confidence.* This is similar to, but different from, esteem. Self-confidence is the product of successes; we have confidence in ourselves when we remember that we succeeded in the past. It goes without saying that we all have failures in life as well as successes, but we can develop the

self-confidence that triggers our success mechanism if we concentrate our thinking on our successes, seeing ourselves at our best time and again. Not that we should deny our failures; this would be unrealistic. We should use our blunders as guides to learning, then forget about them. Then we should bring into our mind images of our triumphs to cement our feeling of confidence in ourselves.

7. *Self-acceptance.* You will not always feel confident; sometimes your stomach will be tied up in knots and perspiration will break out all over your face. Your nervousness will be visible to other people; they may look at you curiously. Or, you may do something rash, injuring your own interests or rudely stepping on someone else's toes. Your imperfections are many—everyone is most imperfect, really —and you must learn to accept this. You must understand that your blunders are *not* your total personality; they are just a part of you, and this is a part which you must accept to be successful. Otherwise you will dedicate your days to an avalanche of self-castigation which will leave you miserable, head bowed, a failure at almost anything you try. You must not look to others for acceptance; this is something you must give yourself.

These are the basic ingredients of the success mechanism. Read them, and reread them. They will help you toward the purposeful execution of your goals. They are success-oriented; they point to goal-attainment, to satisfaction in living.

Creative living today means steering your mind to productive goals.

Humanity—toward Yourself

Of course, you must at all times accept your human weaknesses. This is of tremendous importance to you.

Most people, if they stop to think, understand the plight of underprivileged groups.

Most people, if they pause in the midst of a hectic day, are human toward the problems of their neighbors.

Many people even feel for the frailties and blunders of people they have never met.

And yet these same people, confronted with their own human failings, are—inhuman.

There is no other word for it. Inhuman.

During the Spanish Inquisition of the fifteenth century, Torquemada earned historical infamy for his cruelty.

You, reading this book, do you feel revulsion on seeing his name in print?

But are you more human—toward yourself?

When you stammer during a business conversation, a reflection of tension or confusion—do you forgive yourself?

When you burn the toast and the three-minute eggs are thirteen-minute eggs—do you forgive yourself?

When you misplace a five-dollar bill and lose it—do you forgive yourself?

When you forget an appointment—do you forgive yourself?

When your day goes wrong and you lose your temper and shout and scream—do you forgive yourself?

You must learn to be human toward yourself, to forgive your shortcomings, or your success mechanism will not function and you will attain no goals that will be really satisfying.

Success and self-hate cannot live together. They are enemies, not partners.

When you run the sleep out of your eyes and sit up in bed, tell yourself first thing: Today I will be human—*toward myself*.

The Goal of "Eternal" Youth

In the final analysis, these attitudes of yours toward yourself will be decisive in the success with which you are able to develop your goals.

You must live with yourself and your image of yourself; there is no escape from this. You can travel to Paris or Calcutta, to London or Rome, to Buenos Aires or New Delhi—but you cannot escape. No matter where you are, you take yourself with you. You are your lifelong partner —or enemy.

A wonderful goal whose attainment I wish you is the goal

of feeling youth always—regardless of your chronological age.

I define youth as fresh, vigorous, alive; it is something that bubbles, that does not stagnate.

Beer is youthful when it pours, foaming, from the bottle, full of bounce and zing. It has lost its youth when it is too long uncovered in a glass; it is then inert, it does not gush forth to sparkle.

Youth is song, it is enthusiasm, it is fire. It comes from the spirit, fills the mind, commingles with the success instincts, tingles in the bloodstream.

This is one goal to pursue every day—if only for a few minutes—the goal of feeling youth, for as long as you live.

Think of what you can do to make your days more fun, Use your sense of direction to point the way. Reread the section in this chapter on the success mechanism, and reactivate its operation in you.

Your goal?

More life, more zest, more fun.

Youth—as long as you live.

You must find youth—in you. In your days and years of creative living. In a lifetime of creative living.

This is one of the best goals of all.

· 7 ·

How To Win the
War Against Negative Feelings

YOUR SELF-IMAGE will sustain you in creative living if you learn to declare war on your negative feelings—and win the war in the battlefield of your mind.

Your mind is a battlefield, never doubt this, and if you win, you will experience peace of mind during your fulfilling days.

Your infantry, crawling slowly through the underbrush

seeking contact with the enemy, creeping through the darkness behind his lines to discover his positions, is your awareness of the supreme importance of your thinking and of your mental imaging.

Your air force, equipped with the latest-model jets and tactical striking force, is your adoption of an active philosophy, your setting of goals, your use of your success mechanism. The buildup of your air power is your work to strengthen your self-image, your picture of yourself, your concept of your own worth.

Your navy cannot transport your troops to victory, however, until it has located your great enemy—your failure mechanism. Before you can go forward in this war, you must discover this mechanism of self-defeat and root it out of your mind.

Does this comparison of your thinking with war make you smile? It shouldn't. It shouldn't at all. In our troubled world, so many people's minds are full of misery. To scoop this misery out, to expose the cancerous thoughts to the light, then to crush these morbid ideas and replace them with happy concepts and images—this often requires a war. A very vital war. One, with apologies to Woodrow Wilson, "to make your mind safe for happiness."

Many years ago Edward Bulwer-Lytton said that "The pen is mightier than the sword," and this saying is now almost everyone's cultural heritage.

Today, with the strident advances made in the knowledge of the human mind during the last one hundred years, we can say that *a person's thoughts, his images, are mightier than guns.*

So let us declare war on our negative feelings, on our failure mechanism. But let us resolve that our basic aim is destruction only of negativism—after that, peace and happiness.

Then goals. Goals and full living.

Years of creative living.

Without fear.

Overcoming False Beliefs

We have discussed the significance of goals, but no goal is more vital than to dehypnotize yourself from the false beliefs which paralyze your success mechanism.

You, reading this book, you are a man or a woman—not a god.

What goals are meaningful, what can you do with yourself if your beliefs pull you down into failure? What can you do but sink into the nonactivity of depression, renouncing all goals, blotting sunshine out of your life, moping dejectedly in a dark room while others go out into the world and live?

In creative living you must dehypnotize yourself from your false, negative beliefs about yourself.

The word "dehypnotize" is not too strong because so many people have beliefs which are unshakable, which must be jarred out of them, which only a forceful countersuggestion can uproot. Their beliefs, so often absurd, cement inferiority complexes formed of unfortunate early experiences and ridiculous misinformation.

The results are sad.

Do you believe that your life will be empty because you are an inferior person who has never done anything worthwhile and never will?

Do you believe that you should suffer to atone for the mistakes you've made?

Do you believe that life has no meaning for you because a loved one has passed away?

Do you believe that the only way to live in an atomic age is to spend every day worrying about a nuclear holocaust?

If you think along these or similar lines, you are harboring false beliefs. Granted that you've known tragedy and that you have your faults, you are still hypnotizing yourself with false, negative ideas. Worse, you are torturing yourself with them. You are crucifying yourself; even your worst enemy might be kinder.

In my sixty-five plus years of tenure in this funny world, I have learned some of the most amazing things. One is that people who are completely objective in appraising political trends or medical conditions or stock market movements or mechanical gadgets—*or other people*—are often totally blind to the irrationality of their false beliefs about themselves. Not only that; considerate of others, they can be ruthlessly vindictive toward themselves.

I have operated on dozens and dozens of people to improve deficient features only to find that, after surgery, they replaced this real physical fault in their minds with a nonsensical belief which continued their unswerving fixation on their inferiority. Their negative beliefs varied; their movement toward failure was the same kind of mechanism.

But *your* negative, false belief about *yourself* is true, isn't it? Steve's is laughable and Betty's is idiotic, but yours is true?

Is this what you think?

Then let me tell you a story.

Victory over the "African Bug"

Many years ago, shortly after I opened my office to start practicing as a plastic surgeon, a tall Negro came to see me. Over six feet four inches tall, he towered above me; he complained about his lip.

I examined him (I'll call him Mr. R.). His underlip protruded somewhat, but I could find nothing wrong with it and I told him this.

Mr. R. said that it was not his idea, but his girlfriend's. She had told him that she was ashamed to be seen with him in public because of the protuberance of his lip.

I found him a sweet, dignified giant of a man and thought to myself that a woman in love would never be so critical of such a man.

When I told him this, he still wanted me to perform an operation on his lip. Thinking that an outrageous fee would influence him to forget about a lip operation, I said that it would cost twelve hundred dollars.

Mr. R. said he couldn't afford such a fee and bid me good-bye, thanking me, and bowing in a most courtly manner.

But the next morning he was back, a little black bag in his hand. He dumped its contents on a table. Bills poured out, hundreds and hundreds of bills. Twelve hundred dollars worth of bills—his life savings. He offered them to me most graciously to pay me for operating on his lip.

I was shocked, a little sad too, because I didn't want to deprive him of what was for him a huge sum of money. I told him that I had asked him an exorbitant fee so that he'd give up the idea of a lip operation that he didn't need.

But when he said that he wanted plastic surgery and would go to another doctor if I wouldn't accept him as a patient, I agreed to operate—for a smaller fee and on condition that he tell his "lady love" my fee was twelve hundred dollars.

The operation was simple enough. Under local anesthesia, I cut the superfluous tissue from inside the lip, approximated the rims of the wound with extremely fine silk, and bandaged the lip outside for support. Within half an hour, I was finished. The patient returned a few times to be treated and have the bandages changed; the last one was removed a week later. All the surgery was done inside the lip; there was no visible scar.

Mr. R. was happy with his lip. He crushed my hand in his great grip and thanked me in his hearty, polite tones. Then he strode from my office, a commanding figure.

A few weeks later he was back, but I could hardly recognize him. His body seemed to have shrunk; his hands had lost their strength; his voice was squeaky. I asked him what had happened.

"The bug, sir—the bug!"

"What bug?"

"The African bug, sir," he said. "It's got me, and it's killing me."

He told me his woes. After the bandages on his lip had been removed, he went to see his woman. She had remarked on his new lip and asked him how much it had cost. When he told her "twelve hundred dollars," as I had asked, her whole manner toward him changed. Furious, she accused him of cheating her of the twelve hundred dollars that should have been hers and told him she'd never really loved him. She cursed him and told him that he would die from this curse.

Deeply troubled, R. had gone to his room and lain there for four days. Then he thought of the curse. He was an educated man, had received good schooling; curses and magic were for the ignorant. Still, this woman had held him under her spell from the time he had met her. He figured that if she could put him under a spell when she didn't hate him, then perhaps she could bring on his death with her curse.

Then, running his tongue around, he discovered the horrible thing inside his mouth.

Shortly after this, his landlady, concerned that he was just lying in his room, not eating, brought him a visitor, a "doctor." R. had told him about the terrible thing in his mouth and the "doctor," examining it, cried out as he removed his finger from the thing in R.'s mouth. "It's killing you," he said. "The slimy African bug stuck inside your mouth because of the curse that is on you!"

The tall man, breathing fearfully, covered his face with his hands.

"It is really in your mouth?" I asked him.

"Yes sir." He told me about how the "doctor" tried to help him drive the "African bug" away with liquids, pastes, and potions—but the curse was too strong. Nothing could destroy the "African bug." All he could think of was the "African bug." Fear of the "African bug" kept him awake at night. "It burned inside my lip—"

"Your lip?"

"Yes sir. Inside my mouth."

"You didn't say your *lip* before."

I examined it. "That it?"

He nodded.

"Should I get rid of it?"

"Please sir."

Filling a syringe with Novocain, I injected it in his lip. After the Novocain had taken effect, I removed the "African bug" with knife and forceps. It took a second.

I showed Mr. R. the "African bug" on a piece of gauze; it was no bigger than a grain of rice.

"Is that the bug, sir?" He looked disbelieving.

"It's just a bit of scar tissue which formed on your lip where I removed the stitches after the operation."

"Then there was no African bug?"

I smiled.

Mr. R. stood up. He seemed to have regained his full height in that instant; a rich smile spread over his face and his voice boomed out again as he thanked me in his usual gravely courteous way, bowing as he left.

There was a happy ending to this story; it arrived in the mail. R., enclosing a snapshot of his childhood sweetheart whom he had married, sent me his regards and in a post-script laughed at "African bugs." In the picture he was a smiling, handsome giant of thirty—his true age—with a lovely girl beside him.

What Is Your African Bug?

This story points a fascinating moral. Here is this fine young man, tall and strong, courtly and dignified—unsophisticated, perhaps, but intelligent—yet a ridiculous belief had almost destroyed him.

His fear of the "African bug" is so ridiculous that you may laugh and ask, "How can this possibly apply to me?"

But we all have our "African bugs."

Have you spent your last fifteen years worrying about some catastrophe that has never happened? Then you have an "African bug."

Do you constantly criticize yourself for talking too much or not talking enough or talking incoherently? Is your self-blame so severe that your conversation has become contrived and dead? Then you have an "African bug."

Are you so worried about money that nothing else matters to you? Do you watch your savings account like a Silas Marner, suffering acute indigestion every time you must make a withdrawal, worrying over every dollar that is wasted? Then you have an "African bug."

All these "African bugs" must be brought to light and

exposed for what they are—negative beliefs that pull us down from our true level as human beings, offensive obsessions that disfigure our self-images, that destroy our aspirations for the happiness that is our reasonable expectation.

As in the case of Mr. R., they have a hypnotic effect which must be canceled out. They cause failure. We must wage a relentless war to exterminate them.

Overcoming the Failure Mechanism

Indeed, we must war against all aspects of the "failure mechanism," which is what I call the system of self-reinforcing negative symptoms which can disrupt an unaware individual's positive instincts.

For, just as certain positive predispositions can accelerate the happy functioning of a person's success mechanism, so can negative forces build up with the speed of a rolling stone going downhill, producing chains of negative feedback within the individual which can lead only to defeat.

I like to spell out the components of the failure mechanism, just as I do for the success mechanism, since I feel that this aids people in remembering them. *F*rustration, *A*ggressiveness, *I*nsecurity, *L*oneliness, *U*ncertainty, *R*esentment, *E*mptiness—(F-A-I-L-U-R-E)—these are the elements of the failure mechanism. (I described this mechanism in greater detail in *Psycho-Cybernetics,* hardcover, Prentice-Hall, 1960; paperback, Pocket Books, a division of Simon & Schuster, Inc., 1969.)

These are the enemy; its weapons of destructiveness are horrifying. Let us consider them one by one so that we may penetrate through camouflage to their effect on the human being.

1. *Frustration.* We feel frustration when we fail to achieve important goals or to satisfy basic desires. Everyone feels frustrated now and then because of our imperfect natures and the complex nature of the world; it is chronic frustration which is a symptom of failure. When an individual finds himself caught in a pattern of repeated frustrations, he should ask himself why. Are his goals too perfectionist? Does he block his aims with his own self-criticism? Does he regress

to his feelings as an infant when frustration plus crying resulted in satisfaction? Frustrated rage does not get results; for infants, it may, but not for adults. A morbid concentration on one's grievances with life will only make one's problems more severe. Far better to focus on one's successes, to gain confidence from seeing oneself winning out. Then one can forge ahead in life.

2. *Aggressiveness*. Frustration produces aggressiveness (misdirected). There is nothing wrong with aggressiveness, properly channeled; to reach our goals we must at times be aggressive. But misdirected aggressiveness is a sure-fire symptom of failure, following on the heels of frustration, contributing to a vicious cycle of defeat. It is usually linked up with the setting of inappropriate goals which the individual cannot achieve. This leads to frustrated rage which the person discharges wildly, in all directions, like a mad dog gone berserk or fireworks sputtering into the night. Innocent parties become targets to a person trapped in the frustration-aggression cycle; he may snap at his wife for no reason, bawl out his children, insult his friends, antagonize his co-workers. Furthermore, his rage will increase as his relations with people deteriorate, causing still more frustration and more blind lashing out. Where does this dreadful cycle end? The answer lies not in the elimination of aggression, but in properly channeling it toward the achievement of goals that will bring satisfaction, reducing the unbearable buildup of frustration. The frustrated-aggressive person must see that he can act to reach successes for himself.

3. *Insecurity*. This is another unpleasant feeling; it is based on a feeling of inner inadequacy. When you feel that you do not meet your challenges properly, you feel insecure. Often, however, it is not our inner resources that are lacking; the trouble lies in our setting of perfectionist standards. The insecure person is frequently quite competent but, living with impossible expectations, he tends to criticize himself constantly. His feelings of insecurity cause him to trip himself up so that he falls pathetically short of his true potentials.

4. *Loneliness*. We are all lonely now and then, but I refer here to the extreme feeling of being separated from other people, from yourself, and from life; this is an impor-

tant symptom of failure. Indeed, it is one of the leading failure areas of modern civilization; the commonness of loneliness is enough to fill one's heart with unending sorrow. To know that God's creatures can be so estranged, this is very sad. In Chapter 13 you will find a well-thought-out consideration of the meaning, causes, and solutions of the problem of loneliness.

5. *Uncertainty.* This failure-type symptom is characterized by indecisiveness. The uncertain person believes that if he does not make a decision, he is safe! He is safe from the criticisms he might receive if he took the chance and was proved wrong—safe from the consequences of a decision he made that backfired. This type of person must see himself as perfect; therefore, he cannot afford to be wrong. When a decision is necessary, he looks upon it as a life-or-death decision. If he makes the wrong choice, he will destroy his idealized picture of himself. Therefore, he may dawdle over a trivial decision for long periods of time, wasting his precious hours worrying. When he finally does make up his mind, his decision will be subject to distortions—and he will very likely blunder. The uncertain person cannot live fully because he is afraid to take the plunge and get his feet wet.

6. *Resentment.* This is the excuse-making reaction of the failure-type personality to his status in life. Unable to bear the pain of his failures, he seeks out scapegoats to take the sting out of his own self-blame. Everywhere he finds evidence that life is shortchanging him and he feels resentment; he does not realize that he may be shortchanging himself. But his resentment does not make failure easier to accept; on the contrary, a vicious cycle is set up which involves more frustration and misdirected aggression. Always full of grievances, the resentful person antagonizes other people and thus sets into motion a chain reaction of hatreds. Others dislike his dishonesty, reject his hostility, feel contempt for his self-pity. Chronic resentment leads to self-pity because the resentful person feels he is a victim of injustice. Haven't people blocked his aspirations? Hasn't bad luck entered into the conspiracy to keep him down? The more he pities himself, the more inferior he feels and the more he comes to hate himself and to resent other people—and the world. He does

not realize that his inner resentment is a breeding ground for failure. Only when he sees that he is an actor in life, that he is responsible for setting his goals and channeling his aggression to achieve them, can he break this cycle of failure. Only when he can feel respect for himself, form a realistic image of himself, can he break the habit of resentful thinking which is such a basic component of the failure mechanism.

7. *Emptiness.* Do you know people who are "successful," yet who seem frustrated, resentful, uncertain, insecure, lonely, and misdirectedly aggressive? Then they have achieved success without tools in their hands! Don't be too sure that their "success" is real. For many people gain all the outward signs of success and then feel emptiness because all along the failure mechanism has enmeshed them, and they have really lacked the capacity for creative living. They have made money, but don't know what to do with it. Life is boring to them. They travel here and there, but nowhere can they escape their feeling of emptiness. They feel empty in New York or Paris; they would feel empty in Mars. They have given up on creative goal-striving; they avoid work, shun responsibility. When they wake up in the morning and see the sun, they do not see their opportunities for enjoying the day—instead they worry about what they can do to pass the time. Emptiness is symptomatic of a weak self-image. Having achieved "success," the empty person feels he is a criminal because he thinks he has stolen something that he does not deserve. Thus he feels guilty and turns his victories into failures as he repudiates his creative faculties. His sense of emptiness symbolizes the total operation of his always present failure mechanism.

These are the elements of the failure mechanism; these are the enemy. I have spelled them out for you so that you can remember them easily.

Now, what can you do about them?

How can you win your one great war?

Rising above Failure

To win the war against your enemy—your failure mechanism—you must first be able to pierce the disguises behind which it hides. Plausible rationalizations and seemingly logical thinking may obscure its functioning. Do not fool yourself, or you will lose this wonderful fight for your survival as a contented human being.

You must fire all your emotional artillery at your false beliefs about yourself until you have leveled them to the ground. You must redirect your frustrated aggression and resentment and find ways to surmount your feelings of loneliness and emptiness.

At the same time, let me once again make one point clear: *the act of failing is not a part of the failure mechanism.* The act of failing in some action or project simply means that you are human.

May I assure you of this: If you've never failed at anything, it's a certainty that you never really tried anything.

Or, in the words of the Roman philosopher Seneca, "If thou art a man, admire those who attempt great things, even though they fail."

Was Thomas Edison a failure? Of course not. The thought is absurd. Yet dozens of failures preceded most of his brilliant creations. Edison learned from his failures and built his successes on them.

Discovery is born in error; there are no creations without unsuccessful experiments.

This sums up one of the chief lessons that I have learned from life: that blunders, errors in judgment and in application, are unavoidable unless you retreat from life into a state of apathy—and, even then, in your inertia you'll make mistakes. *The secret of successful living is to rise above your failures to your good moments.* This is the key concept, to forget your errors, to stop grieving over them, to have compassion for your own human fallibility. Then, unburdened with guilt, you can step out determinedly into the world, seeing yourself at your best, formulating your goals, and bringing out into the game of life your success instincts.

This principal is especially applicable when you try new things. For, when you experiment, you are bound to make mistakes. Never deny your mistakes; admit them freely. But learn to minimize these mistakes, to be as tolerant toward yourself as you would be toward a friend, or you must throttle your experimentation.

Then you can rise to your true potential as a human being and make each year the enriching vindication of your individuality that it should be.

Exercise 6

Every day examine the negative beliefs which pull you down.

Do you feel that you are stupid?

Are you obsessed with the feeling that you are ugly?

Or do you destroy yourself with the allegation that you are weak?

Unmasculine?

Unfeminine?

Undeserving of anything good?

These are a few choice areas for self-torture.

I don't know what negative beliefs you use to undermine yourself; you must ferret them out for yourself.

Your exercise is this: Let's think about these self-destroying thoughts and see if we can do something about them (even if you're positive that you're just no good) because I assure you that your thinking is irrational.

Irrational thinking has run berserk down through history. We have had medicine men, alchemists, gold rushes, haunted houses, expeditions after a "fountain of youth"—not to speak of the brutal wars that have bloodied the pages of history books. For many years there were outrageous beliefs about women thought to be "witches." "Witches" were burned in Europe: Joan of Arc was executed as a "witch," and in the United States we had the shameful episode in Salem, in which a number of "witches" were put to death.

Yet, sad to say, many of us today treat ourselves as if we were "witches."

In examining your accusations against yourself, let's see if you are not being unfair.

If you castigate yourself as "stupid," on what do you base this charge? Granted that you've been unwise, perhaps many times, have you *never* been wise? Have you never been shrewd? Have you never been intelligent? Then your self-criticism is basically self-mutilation. What it comes down to is that you feel you have no rights; you believe in short-changing yourself.

Examine the "African bugs" which plague you. There might be a grain of reality to them—just as there was a bit of scar tissue in Mr. R.'s mouth. But are these the devastating indictments that you build them into? No, this is irrational thinking.

People are people. The strong are weak, and the weak are strong.

Some low-to-medium IQ people have rare common sense.

Some homely-looking women are devoted friends—and can look beautiful.

Some people with physical handicaps are most compassionate.

Some emotionally unstable people are extremely brilliant.

Psychologists have found that many adult stutterers will talk fluently when they are talking to children.

Some criminals can become responsible members of society if someone will give them a helping hand.

These are grays; there are no blacks-and-whites. But what do you do to yourself with your negative beliefs? You make yourself all evil, all thumbs, all negating.

Everyone knows defeat at times. Joe Louis was for years heavyweight champion; in his prime he was almost invincible, a symbol of power.

Yet when he first tried boxing, Louis was bumbling, awkward. Unknown amateurs beat him time and again. In one amateur bout he was knocked down nine times in one fight.

Now that you've examined your negative beliefs about yourself and are in the process of reducing them to reasonable proportions, let's see if you can't discard them. If you can't, at least maintain them at reasonable dimensions so that you can live with them.

Go to the next step now, and repicture a success, one that you're really proud of.

Fill your mind with it, see it, smell it, feel it, grab hold of this success picture and hold it in your mind.

When the critical thoughts counterattack, kick them out and come back, once again, with the good self-image—in technicolor.

To live creatively, you must win this war in your mind. Don't give up! Keep fighting, and chances are you will win.

Say to yourself: "I shall concentrate on the confidence of my past successes, not on my past failures. I deserve the good things in life. I am the captain of my ship, and I shall steer my mind to a productive goal."

Your Pacemaker

You've read about the man with the pacemaker who is living so graciously; learn a lesson from this man.

Let your self-image be the pacemaker of your heart, your mind, and your soul. Each day reactivate your successful instincts until the success habit becomes part of you, until it hypnotizes you—for, after all, habit is a form of self-hypnosis.

Work hard to banish negative beliefs, to exterminate the seeds of loneliness. Work hard, it is not easy. But you can do it.

War is hellish and if your mind is deeply entrenched in negative concepts, you will have to struggle fiercely to win your battle. But it is a battle worth winning.

So that you can live creatively—with joy.

So that you can laugh and sing and walk the streets proudly in broad daylight.

You've read about "Wingy," who refused to let her handicap stop her from living.

Think of her and resolve to be as determined to succeed as she. Let this thought be your pacemaker.

Let your strengthened self-image inspire you to move forward into a more vital way of life.

Belief, belief in yourself, that is the best pacemaker of all.

· 8 ·

How To Accept Pleasure

A MAN SITS at his desk; he is a key executive for a large corporation.

His desk is full of memos, letters, contracts, other papers. Two lights on the side of his telephone flicker on and off, indicating people waiting to talk to him. He is in conference with two men who sit, smoking, waiting for his attention. He looks at his appointment book and notes that another vital conference is set for this day, that he is lunching with the president of the company, and that he must devote a few hours to a project which is behind schedule. Also, he must dictate letters to A, B, and C and also . . .

The enormity of these pressures might overwhelm many of us. "It's too much for us," we'd say.

But not this man. He feels . . . pleasure.

He refuses to let a morbid imagination ruin his effectiveness. Instead he sees in his mind the successes that his day will bring.

He turns cordially to his visitors, listens attentively, does his best to respond to their needs and demands. He answers the phone and, getting to the heart of the communicating instantly, returns to his visitors. He tells them what action he intends to take on the matters under discussion, dictates a message into a machine, turns back to them to ask if they are happy with his decisions. They are, and he ushers them to the door, shaking hands warmly. Nothing phony; simple pleasure in a direct, effective moving toward goals.

This man projects his imagination into action in a positive way. He accepts his right to feel happy and successful.

Many people, however—this includes many executives —use their imaginations to block themselves from pleasure, and this can be tragic.

Many adults fill their minds with morbid, depressing thoughts—and pleasure is caught in a squeeze in which it is crushed. They worry about disasters that never—or rarely —happen. The feelings of pleasure and satisfaction from their work are not tolerated, and they obviously cannot function in the successful way that this executive does.

They do not enjoy their work; they do not enjoy their "play" either.

Epicurus, the Greek philosopher whose doctrines became known as Epicureanism, believed that "we call pleasure the alpha and omega of a blessed life. Pleasure is our first and kindred good."

Closer to the present, Sydney Smith, an English clergyman who was also known as a wit, wrote, "Man could direct his ways by plain reason, and support his life by tasteless food, but God has given us wit, and flavour, and brightness, and laughter, and perfumes, to enliven the days of man's pilgrimage, and to charm his pained steps over the burning marle."

Yet many of us endure existences that contain little if any pleasure; the "food" is "tasteless" and the thoughts are like poison swirling around the mind. There is heartache and there is misery, but where is the joy? Where is the singing? There is complaining and whining, but where is the gladness?

You *can* feel pleasure. You can sing in the shower and feel musical thoughts in your mind and givingness in your heart—it is a question, basically, of what you will allow yourself.

You must not block the attainment of your legitimate satisfactions. No years can be creative if they deny the principle of happiness.

Pleasant Living Today

Living today should mean pleasure, but our modern concept of living is often just the reverse—negative in concept and implying the renunciation of one's self-image. Modern living often means renouncing satisfaction because of a phantom known as "twentieth-century anxieties."

Living should be a happy vocation. People should be useful to themselves and to others. Pleasure must be part of us—like our heart, our eyes, our hands, our feet. It should know no race, no creed, no color, no status, no age. The good feelings in life belong to us and there is no moral aspect to it except that it is immoral for people to fester in unhappiness.

Forgetting the mistakes of the past, you can live each day to the full. You can find pleasures in doing, in living, in friendships . . . if you feel that you have a right to enjoy yourself. I make this qualification because so many people do not give themselves this simple right.

I am not a great believer in sin, but if there *is* sin, it is for people to sit around upbraiding themselves for mistakes they've made, mistakes which are only human.

I know so many people who do this, who waste the wonderful power of their imaginations torturing themselves with their crimes. It is sad but true that many of you who blame yourselves so severely have in reality led lives characterized by hard effort and a constant attempt to be decent human beings; yet you give yourselves no rights.

Recently I went to Oklahoma to lecture to a group of convicts in a large prison. I spoke individually to a few of them without knowing their specific crimes, but surely some were robbers, forgers, assaulters. Enemies of society, trying to pull themselves together, they had made horrendous mistakes—but I doubt if they blamed themselves as much as some of you people who have lived comparatively blameless lives.

When you criticize yourself, you deny yourself pleasure. Yet you have the right to feel free of fear, to feel free of guilt—to feel pleasure.

In one sense, creative living involves a resolution within

one's mind to be happy. It is a victory of one's positive thinking-imaging forces over one's negative thinking-imaging forces. You prepare for creative living as you strengthen your image of yourself each day; you live vitally, allowing yourself pleasure because you feel that you deserve it.

A Fresh Look at Living

I have read other books on creative living. Many advise you about what to do and where to go and what agencies to consult for this and that.

You might continue to wonder about this book, you might continue to say to yourself, "But where are the specific suggestions? Why doesn't the author tell us where to go and what to do?"

Ah, but I am! Not geographically, not vocationally— but in your mind, where it counts.

If this book helps you in your day-to-day living, it will be because it is nonspecific, *because it doesn't tell you what to do,* because it focuses on the one area which you must understand is all-important—the area of your mind and its thinking and imaging processes.

To live creatively, *you* must allow *yourself* happiness. *You.* You must do it. Your self-image. Your self-image must be strong enough so that you sustain this feeling of pleasure.

I could advise you to become a doctor or a lawyer or a salesman, but when you find yourself, you will, if you're still young, find your proper vocation.

I could advise you to go to Florida or California—I know nothing bad about Florida or California and the climate is usually pleasant—but is this basic to your happiness? You take with you to Florida or California or Rome or Paris or Hawaii—you name it—yourself and, while external factors may have some importance, it is basically your mental concepts which will bring you happy living or boring days.

I hope that, after reading this book, you will apply its concepts to help you plan years of pleasure. In part, this is a selfish wish, since knowing that I have been useful would give me pleasure. You cannot touch these ideas, as you could a sofa or a chair, but ideas can create infinitely more contentment—even though they are invisible.

Through strengthening your self-image, through seeing yourself at your best, through encouraging your success instincts, you can create pleasure for yourself.

But the unfortunate fact is that many people do not feel that it would be fair for them to be happy. They do not feel they deserve it, and they use rationalizations to explain their misery.

If only they had money . . .

If not for that financial catastrophe . . .

If that accident hadn't happened . . .

If not for that childhood disease which only they had contracted . . .

A tragic event from the past is dredged up, and this is used to explain all the pain, all the lack of pleasure.

But what they don't realize is that everyone knows tragedy, everyone knows pain, fate did not single them out for punishment. Successful, happy people know pain, too, but they just keep pushing forward—through pain to pleasure.

Success from Failure

Suppose you knew a man who'd been seriously ill with scarlet fever as a child, almost completely deaf from the beginning of his adolescence. At the age of six, he set fire to his father's barn, accidentally, and the fire almost spread to the entire town in which he lived—luckily the wind did not fan the flames; for this carelessness his father whipped him in public, as an example to the other children.

His family was poor and so he went to work at the age of twelve. On one job he started another fire, and more than once he was discharged because he refused to accept discipline. At one point, alone in New York City, he was so poverty-stricken that he subsisted for days and days on one five-cent meal (apple dumplings and coffee).

Knowing this background, would you suspect that this one of the most influential men who ever lived?

Who was he? I'll give you another hint—from an earlier

chapter. He had only three months of formal education in his entire life.

That's right—Thomas Edison.

This is the imaginative marvel who between 1869 and 1910 applied for well over one thousand different patents for his inventions.

This is the man who found much pleasure in work, who found time to father six children, who did not let his deprivations defeat him, who never stopped living fully, utilizing his own individual gifts to the full.

This is the genius, the creator of so much in modern civilization, who, on his seventy-fifth birthday, asked his ideas on life, answered that he believed in work, in using nature for man's pleasure. He added that, at seventy-five, he had a backlog of inventions he was planning that would keep him busy for another hundred years.

In his eighties Edison was conducting experiments with rubber inspired by manufacturer Harvey Firestone.

At eighty-four, after nearly dying, he went back to his work, before his final collapse brought grief to mankind.

With the passing of time, as other men's fame shrinks, Edison's grows—such was the scope of his overwhelming accomplishments.

Yet how many people are there who would find in his early difficulties good excuse for denying themselves creative satisfaction—and all pleasures—for a lifetime?

How many would say they were unlucky and renounce their basic winning instincts?

Somewhere Edison was able to find within himself the self-belief that kept him going through times of trouble into days of pleasure.

This feeling—one of deserving—is what we must all find in ourselves.

You Can't Retire from Life

When I was in medical school, more than forty years ago, a fellow student named Mickey was hospitalized with a severe case of influenza. He almost died from the disease, which was much more serious then than it is today.

He recovered partially from the disease—his condition was no longer critical—but his recovery was not complete.

My fellow students and I would visit him at the hospital; it was extremely depressing. Formerly husky and energetic, with bristling blond hair, Mickey was pale, had lost much weight, and he still *looked sick*. His skin was pale, his eyes were depressed; the life was gone from them. You felt when you saw him that he envied you your own health, and I would feel uncomfortable talking to him at his bedside.

We took turns visiting him.

Then one day there was a sign on his closed door: NO VISITORS.

We were alarmed—but there was no cause. Mickey's life was not in danger.

Mickey had asked the doctor to put the sign up. The visits of his friends and relatives had not cheered him up. Instead, they had made him feel more glum. He wanted nothing to do with us.

Later, Mickey told us how he felt during these days when he wanted nothing to do with the world of people. He felt scornful toward everybody and everything, feeling that each of us was worthless or ridiculous as a person. He told us that, in the prison of his mind, no one escaped the lash of his criticism; he just wanted to be left alone with the misery of his thoughts.

There was no pleasure in him. Depressed by his physical deterioration, he felt rejection of life grow in him until he renounced the world.

These were truly days of no-pleasure for Mickey. His resentment was too great for *him* to tolerate.

But he was lucky.

The day nurse, understanding his state of mind, decided to help him.

One day, after some tricky preludes, she told him that there was a girl patient who was suffering emotionally; Mickey could lift her spirits if he would write her love letters.

Mickey wrote her one letter, then two. He pretended that he had seen her briefly one day and that he had thought about her ever since. After they were both well, he wrote, perhaps they could take walks in the park together.

Mickey felt pleasure in writing these letters—for the first time in many days—and his health began to improve. He wrote many letters and was walking briskly, spiritedly, around his room. Soon he would be discharged from the hospital.

This knowledge saddened him because he had never seen the girl. So much pleasure from writing of his adoration, a glow of love would come to his face at the thought of her, but he had never seen her—not even once!

Mickey asked the nurse if he could visit her in her room. The nurse approved and gave him the room number —414.

But there was no such room.

There was no such girl.

And Mickey learned the truth—that the nurse had done her best to make him well. Seeing his gloom, sensing his critical, hating thoughts toward everyone, she felt that to recover from his physical illness he needed pleasure in his life.

She sensed that what Mickey needed to give him pleasure was the opportunity to give—to someone he could give to, a fellow patient, a fellow sufferer. She told him about this imaginary girl and . . .

So Mickey left the hospital, wiser, knowing in his heart the futility of resentment—and the happiness one gets from giving.

He told us the story, for we were once again his friends.

Mickey told it to us contentedly. His eyes gleamed, his cheeks were afire because he knew how it felt to escape from the dark world of self-inflicted gloom into the sunny world where one can live with pleasure.

Exercise 7

So where, then, is the road to pleasure? Is there such a road—or is it a dead end?

Pleasure is a reality for those fearlessly oriented in its direction, those for whom it is a legitimate aim.

If, like Mickey did, you turn away from the world with disappointment, then you renounce all chance of pleasure;

you turn your back on it, *you* uproot it from your feelings, *you* destroy it even where you find it.

You must encourage your tendencies toward happiness.

These ideas will help you to find pleasure in your life. Sit in a comfortable chair and read them over and over until they become a part of your thinking. Sit, think, enjoy.

1. *Work to build up your self-image.* There is no pleasure if you do not like your image of yourself; you cannot live on the top floor of a building which has no foundation. You will not find pleasure in work, in travel, in conversation, in power, in money, or in beautiful scenery—if your self-image is inadequate. Search around in your mind each day for your successful memories—get into the habit of searching for these wonderful moments—and bring these realistically happy times front stage center. See yourself this way, successful, acting and thinking the way you like to act and think; reactivate these positive images each day. Not only must you focus on your picture of contentment, but you must also be kind to your areas of weakness if pleasure is to be a factor in your life. This building up of your self-image, make it a daily habit of prime importance; pleasure starts with yourself.

2. *Unearth your hidden wealth.* What is this hidden wealth? It is your creative gifts, your talents, your abilities for doing and for giving—but why do you keep them hidden? Is it because you fear criticism or because your resources, unused to exposure, may seem imperfect? Almost every person alive has some area of excellence, some aptitudes the expression of which make him feel more alive, more important as a person; what a pity that so much of this self-expression is wasted! For undeveloped resources have no more value than unmined, buried precious metals. If you cannot reach them and bring them into the open, others do not even know they exist. Worse still, even you do not know of their existence and, in your ignorance, you deprive yourself of so much pleasure. You don't need shovels or bulldozers, land titles or contracts to unearth your precious gifts; all you need is the determination that you are going to give yourself and your spirit the same loving attention that you would to the treasures of your material

world: your automobile or your front lawn or your kitchen.

3. *Give to others*. This is a world in which sometimes the only thing that seems to matter is the "fast buck." Giving to others is less important, it may seem, than keeping one step ahead of them; this is one of the great tragedies of civilized life today. Yet most people, even if they won't admit it, have a tremendous craving for love and acceptance; they also long to express their goodness, to give of themselves. Through careful, considerate treatment may surprise most people and even arouse their suspicions, if they feel that your friendliness is genuine, they will respond warmly. If they have long felt deprived of affection, the extent of their gratitude may amaze you. In helping others, you may find the greatest satisfactions you have ever known.

4. *Concentrate on your goals*. As I said in Chapter 3, you must have goals for everyday living. It is not enough to select goals; your next step is to focus your attention on them with a steady gaze, then reach them. This is the only way to get real enjoyment from your life activities. Do you like to play golf? Then *play* golf, don't just dabble at it. When you're driving off the tee or putting, don't think about the office or your income tax; keep your mind on your putting and your driving, look at the ball, study the terrain, measure each blade of grass—like a professional out to win the big money. The point is not just that you'll play better golf; it's that you'll gain more pleasure from playing. The same thing applies to anything you do—painting, cooking, writing, singing, planning something, swimming, building a table, feeding your dog—you must lose yourself in it. Concentration on something you like will fill your world with pleasure.

Bending Habit to Your Will

This exercise should help you to adjust your sights so that you can penetrate to the heart of what spells out happiness for you. Work on it daily if but for a few moments, reorientating your thinking toward values that will help you.

It should also help you to bypass some pitfalls that bar the way to contented living.

Negative habits are your deadly enemy; you may get accustomed to distasteful ways of thinking and doing things which you cannot change without great effort. You may find yourself gravitating into worried thinking or into inconsiderate relating to other people or into other habitual patterns that may turn you away from pleasure.

How can you break bad habits?

I'll tell you about a bad habit of mine, and how I broke it.

There is invariably a doctor's dressing room alongside the hospital operating room, and before an operation, I would go there to change from my clothes into surgical operating garb. I would strip in front of a locker and stand there, just shoes and socks on. Then I would roll my money into a tight wad of bills and stuff it into my left sock. I developed this habit as a poverty-stricken intern, when the loss of a dollar was a minor catastrophe; the lockers were no protection since there were no locks.

Anyway, this became a habit with me; for perhaps thirty years, I stuffed my money into my left sock before operating. After awhile I did it unconsciously; since I like to operate early in the morning, the dressing room is usually empty, and no one ever told me how funny it looked. A thirty-year habit, and what a habit!

Until a few years ago, another doctor saw me and stared, amazed. He tried manfully to hide a chuckle, but he was too amused.

I took stock of myself then. Upon reflection, I decided that this was a most eccentric habit, which I would change.

But the next time, and the next, I rolled my money into my sock. When a habit takes hold, it is hard to break.

When I pinned the money inside my jacket, it didn't stop me. Without thinking, I unpinned it and put it inside my left sock.

Nothing worked. Day after day I would operate, my dollar bills snug in my sock.

Finally, I got an idea. I bought a mirror and fitted it inside my locker door. Then I got undressed in front of the mirror and watched as I took the money and placed it inside my left sock. *Seeing* myself worked wonders. "How ridiculous I am!" I thought and laughed and laughed. I couldn't look at myself without laughing; what an absurd habit, I thought; no wonder the other doctor had to hide his amusement.

After seeing my habit, I never did it again. Finally, I was free of it; the mirror had helped me to see its absurdity.

Now, how about your bad habits—habits more crippling, perhaps, because they may stand between you and pleasure?

Do you need a mirror to change them?

Not necessarily.

But you do need a mirror in your mind so that you can see yourself as objectively as others see you, so that you can see the habits, often unconscious, which may keep you from the good things of life.

Do you have the habit of looking to the other person to talk instead of asserting your own opinion?

Do you habitually shrink from an excursion that's fun because you might get sunstroke or frostbite, or it might rain and you'll get wet?

Or are you a habitual loser because you plunge too fast, without looking over the odds, surveying the terrain?

Hold up your inner mirror and look at your negative habits; you might not put your money in your left sock, but you might do other silly things which keep you from pleasure.

Hard as it is, you can break habits. You can change, and you can be happy if you *see* and if you are determined to succeed and if you are willing to work hard.

Pleasure Every Day for You

One more suggestion: *Do not set conditions for your pleasure.*

Do not say, "I'll have fun when I make $10,000."

Or "The happiness will come when I get on that plane to Paris and Rome and Vienna."

Or "When I'm sixty-five and I retire, I'll just lie in a deck chair in the sunshine and . . ."

There should be no *ifs* about it.

Each day a basic goal must be your feeling that you

deserve to enjoy yourself, whether you're a millionaire or a pauper.

A millionaire with a weak self-image can say to himself, "Someone will steal all my money and then nobody will talk to me."

A poor man with a strong self-image can say to himself, "While my creditors are chasing me around the block, I'll enjoy the exercise."

Don't kid yourself; if you really want happiness in your life, you will find it—if you can live with good fortune.

I can't repeat this last phrase often enough: *if you can live with good fortune.*

Because I have known so many people who couldn't live with happiness. After a great success, instead of relaxing, their anxieties would intensify. Everything and everyone seemed to be chasing them—diseases, lawsuits, accidents, Internal Revenue, even relatives—in their minds. They could not relax at all until they once again tasted what they were really looking for—*failure.*

Court pleasure, not pain. Pay homage to its virtues; feel that you are worthy.

Find pleasure in the little things: food that tastes delicious, friendship that is sincere, a sun that is warning, a smile that is meant to cheer.

In *Othello* the sophisticated, worldly wise William Shakespeare wrote, "Pleasure and action make the hours seem short."

Short or long, make your hours ring and bubble with pleasure.

Laugh at those who say that pleasure is not part of life, because they are ignorant; but forgive them, because they are not as wise as you.

For, if you've read this far, you know that this is not so.

You know that happiness is real.

You know that happiness is a gift that you give yourself —not just during Christmas, but all year round.

Instant Confidence:
That Inner Creative Force

THESE ARE push-button times, and our demands are often met in an instant.

We have instant coffee, for one thing, and products from orange juice to frozen vegetables to frozen dinners slide from refrigerator to table to our palates almost constantly.

"Instant" is a key twentieth-century word; we save time and energy if we are in tune with the miracles of modern industry—and almost everyone is.

Flick a switch of your television set, and in seconds you see pictures of the wars, the riots, the disasters, the public figures which make the daily newspaper headlines in our dramatic world.

Push another button and music fills your room—in an instant.

Many people are skeptical of the benefits of all these instant mechanisms; they wonder if this "progress" is really regression—I myself sometimes question the too-packaged, too-glib, too-instant quality of some of our super-civilized "comforts."

But this chapter is about instant confidence—and this quality is something we all need, no matter who we are, no matter what our age and our status in life.

It is an inner fire, a quick-flowing sureness that can make our hearts sing, building the positive habits that will flow smoothly into fresh, crisp living.

We all have instant confidence within us, waiting to be used. In our lives we have known failures, successes, and mixed experiences. If we minimize the failures, resolving to rise above them and make a habit of drawing upon the confidence of past successes, seeing them in our minds, tasting them again and again, humbly, not boastfully, self-confidence becomes second nature to us, a treasure trove waiting to be tapped the instant we want it. Repeating, revisualizing, reemphasizing the winning moments creates in us an ongoing drive—instant confidence.

It is debatable, perhaps, whether your coffee is better slow-brewed or instant. It is also debatable whether your orange juice is better squeezed by hand or instant.

But there is nothing debatable about instant confidence. It is a value to those who feel it; it is a priceless value, there can be no doubt of this.

You need this feeling of belief in yourself, this instinctive feeling of belief in yourself, to fully utilize your resources, so that you can constructively plunge forth into life activities.

You need this feeling to accelerate you forward into a dynamic pattern of living.

The Birth of the "Born Orator"

Not too many months ago I lectured in New York's Town Hall on the self-image. As I stood on the raised platform, I faced the hundreds and hundreds of people in the audience without fear. I spoke for fifty minutes but, when it was over, it seemed to me like ten or fifteen minutes. I felt myself propelled, an inner force guiding me through my lecture, surely, enjoyably. I made no mistakes, speaking off the cuff with only a short outline, and felt no need to pause. The words flowed from me naturally. Afterward, someone in the audience clasped my hand and said, "Doctor, you're a born orator."

I thanked him for his compliment, but actually this was not the truth at all. I was not a *born* orator.

Months later I addressed an audience of close to two thousand people, lecturing on the success mechanism. I spoke for an hour, but again it seemed like fifteen minutes, and I felt as relaxed as if I were talking to a few friends at home; once more I felt an inner force guiding me. Later a woman thanked me and said, "You are a born orator."

I did not correct her, but it had not always been this way with me. Not at all.

In Miami Beach, I spoke to well over a thousand people on the overcoming of loneliness. Once more I felt no fear, and my hour in the spotlight seemed to fly by. Relaxed, I sang in my questionable singing voice, and the people joined me in singing. I felt at home; more, I felt *good*. I was living, really living. A reverend congratulated me later and said, "You should be ordained as a minister. You're a born orator."

The following day, in Miami Beach, one of the speakers scheduled to address the Congress fell ill, and I took his place on a few minutes' notice. Without notes I addressed my audience and felt up to the challenge. I did not falter. I felt in rapport with the people listening to me, and I did not feel self-conscious; my confidence did not desert me.

What is the point of these stories? Am I exhibiting myself narcissistically, smiling at myself in the mirror, boasting about how marvelous I am?

Not at all. This is not my intention in the slightest. Because truly I was not a "born" orator.

On the contrary, I had known terrible failures in this area.

Let me tell you a story about myself when I was younger.

By nature I'm shy and sensitive, and when I was a second-year medical student one of the required courses—on pathology, or diseases of the tissues—was a nightmare. When the professor would call upon me to stand up and recite, I would feel panic. I would look at him, thinking he was angry with me and wanted me to fail. My eighty fellow-students seemed 160 angry eyes; I thought that they wanted me to fail, too.

And that is what I did. I just couldn't gather my thoughts and give the right answers and I would sit down, feeling crushed. *I know my subject,* I would insist to myself. *Why can't I give the right answers when everyone is watching?* Time after time I failed my oral quizzes, hating myself for my incompetence.

I lived for days and weeks with the fear that I would flunk the subject. I wanted very much to be a doctor; I could not let this happen to me.

Then, taking a written examination in pathology, I stumbled onto an invaluable insight. Examining slides under the microscope, we had to identify the specimens. The situation was different now. The professor and students did not exist to me; I did not see their faces; the only thing that mattered to me was the slide I saw under the microscope. I knew my subject and felt no terror. I answered the questions; my grade was "A."

I knew nothing then of psycho-cybernetics or self-image psychology. All I knew was that I had a tremendous desire to be a doctor, that nothing would stop me from my achieving my ambition. I realized that I had succeeded on the written exams through ignoring the presence of the professor and eighty students. I said to myself, "Next time the professor calls on me in front of the class, I will hear the question, but I will pay no attention to the large audience. I will not see them, I will make believe I'm looking through a microscope at a slide."

And the most remarkable thing happened. Relaxed, I answered surely. I had canceled out my fears, blotted out my negative feelings, and I passed the course with honors. Drawing on the confidence I felt in my written examination, I substituted it for the fear I felt during oral examinations. With such confidence, used instantly, when I needed it, and knowing my subject, I spoke well and licked my agonizing problem.

Yes, this was my beginning as a "born orator."

The Habit of Confidence

The years passed. I was a plastic surgeon now. I knew my work thoroughly. I operated often and my operations were professional. There was no panic. I had trained myself to use my self-confidence, to rise above fear, and as the years passed confidence became a habit with me—second nature—that I could call upon and use at a moment's notice, *instantly. Instant confidence* born of continuous repetition!

In the quiet of the operating room, I trained groups of men in plastic reconstructive surgery, and afterward I spoke to them, calm and relaxed, in the doctor's quarters. I knew my work and taught others. I was confident, and they learned.

And then I said to myself, "Wouldn't it be a wonderful goal to achieve—to write a book for people with normal faces who have an inner scar—a fear, a frustration, a hurt feeling, a guilt—teaching them to be their own plastic surgeon, without a knife—a special kind of plastic surgeon who, with compassion for themselves, would remove their inner scars by utilizing the confidence within them by declaring war on negative feelings—as I did in the class on pathology in medical school." That is how my book *Psycho-Cybernetics* came into being.

Later, when I was called upon to lecture to large groups of people, I remembered the days when I spoke all flustered in my class in pathology. I then forgot these failures and rose above them to remember my successful recitations and to the later days when I spoke calmly and clearly to the students studying plastic surgery with me. I spoke to large groups in a huge auditorium as if I were talking to a few friends in my living room.

I spoke well, without fear, and today I lecture to hundreds and thousands of people in many different parts of the world: in churches, temples, colleges, to sales executives, insurance executives, all sorts of businessmen and professional men, telling them about the potential power in their self-image. And I'm considered a born orator.

Am I? Of course not. You've read my story.

Naturally, *you* don't have to be an orator or talk before huge groups of people. What I do advise you to do is to talk to yourself now and then, take stock of yourself, see where you're going. I say to you that if I could rise above panic in my life, you can in your life. You remember the confidence of your past successes—no matter how few—and you dwell on these happy moments. You reenact these successes again and again in your mind, seeing them and smelling them, until they become part of you—like brushing your teeth and tying your shoelaces before leaving your home to face the world. You get into the habit of tapping this inner force of confidence instantly when necessary—and it's necessary every moment of the day. This, then, becomes instant confidence and it is a feeling of winning life's many small battles.

I wrote that when I spoke to a good-sized audience, it suddenly seemed to me that some inner force was guiding me through my lecture. What was really guiding me was the inner force of instant confidence that I tapped instinctively. This subconsciously reactivated the success mechanism within me.

This confident feeling confirms your use of the success mechanism within you—within all of us. And in using this confidence repeatedly, you have subconsciously called upon all the other aspects of the success mechanism: your sense of direction, your goal before you, your understanding of the situation. You have used your courage, your compassion, your self-respect, your conviction that you are *somebody* who can amount to *something*. You have accepted yourself for what you are, and you have made your self-image rise as tall as you want it to be. You have refused to destroy yourself with negative feelings—as I did when I was studying pathology. You have refused to let fear and frustration sidetrack you from your goal. You have refused to permit frustration, resentment, hurt feelings, loneliness, and emptiness to throttle you. You insist on expressing yourself until you reach self-fulfillment. You show the greatest expression of confidence at the very moment of discouragement when, with courage, you start again, turning a crisis into an opportunity. This is what instant confidence is. It is a winning surge.

With instant confidence you prepare yourself for success, putting a smile on your self-image. Your self-image is at its best. You have cancelled out the obstacles in reaching your goal. You've put a creative tattoo on the tape recorder of your brain, reactivating it creatively when needed, replaying it when necessary, making a habit of success. You have used worry as a challenge by turning negative feelings into positive ones; through worry you have cultivated courage and faith. You have overcome despair with hope.

The choice is up to you; you must utilize the worthwhile creative instinct within you to *succeed*—not fail.

In the process of acquiring instant confidence, you can change the old recordings of past blunders, concentrating on your winning feelings. You can substitute a new record for an old one.

Instant confidence means keeping your eye on the ball, getting more living out of life and more life in your years. It is the spirit of youth within you—within all of us—if we look for it and cultivate it and work at it.

A Lady with Instant Confidence

Many years ago I answered the telephone to hear a voice of sheer music. The woman who serenaded me, in prose, told me that she had read one of my books back home in her native country (South Africa) and that she had enjoyed it so much that she wanted to meet me. Perhaps I would even autograph her book for her.

Her charm flowed across the wires and I could not help being deeply intrigued. Her voice was magnetic; you felt immediately her confidence in herself, and this sureness seemed to mellow her voice so that she seemed to be almost singing.

I was not operating that afternoon and, giving in to a surge of intense curiosity, I invited her to come to tea—that afternoon.

Her name was Carolyn Nesbitt.

She was just as I'd pictured her.

She was elderly—in her seventies?—but she was youth itself.

Her hair was silver, but her eyes were young and bright. Her frame was fragile, but her face glistened with interest in life.

In an old-world way, she was utterly charming. She expressed admiration for my furnishings, and her voice was melodic, her eyes were clear and smiling.

And so we talked.

In my book I had written about two romances in my life which had not worked out. She said she had been fascinated with these passages, and expressed compassion for the sorrow I had undoubtedly undergone.

Then she told me about a man she had loved, who had married another woman. Afterward, she had fallen in love with her husband—who had since died—and raised a large family. For a while, though, she had been heartbroken.

She wrenched from me the admission that I was not married.

She itemized the fruits of her marriage: seven children, in all corners of the globe, plus twelve grandchildren. Six of the seven children were married. The other, an unmarried daughter, lived in New York where I practiced as plastic surgeon.

She suggested that I meet her unmarried daughter, whose charms she rhapsodized over, who was a lovely person, interested in writing just as I was.

I have never claimed to be a genius, but the purpose of her visit became clear to me, as over and over words like "romance" and "marriage" floated bell-like in the air and and hung there, over us, so appealingly.

I did not choose to succumb to her matchmaking, but I did not resent it at all. On the contrary, I admired her charming, sure semi-directness.

After she had left, friendly and sweet, I thought about the whole episode and felt continued admiration. In her later years, Mrs. Nesbitt had pursued, halfway around the world, her ardent, goal-oriented matchmaking. Reading my book in South Africa, she had seized upon me as a possible husband for her daughter and seen her manipulation through—with gentility and givingness.

After New York she said she would see her *married* son Charles in Winnipeg, Canada, and then she would see her *married* daughter Mary in London. The following year there was a *married* daughter Elizabeth to see in Rio de Janeiro and a *married* son Ronald in New Zealand. For Charles's son and Mary's daughters and Elizabeth's twin boys, as well as Ronald's two boys and one girl, were reaching *marriageable* ages.

I sat alone, relaxing, and laughed. I wished her good hunting.

Then I laughed again. But not at her—with her.

I wished her good luck in her flights around the world, a nightingale singing of love and marriage, a nightingale in her later years, serenading in her voice so sweet and lovely.

Your Great Inner Force

Why do I tell this story?

That's easy.

Not to write about marriage, *not* to ramble purposelessly, *not* to tell a meaningless, but fascinating anecdote.

I tell you about it because this woman had within her an intangible, yet supremely important, force which translated itself in her personality into—instant confidence.

It was her self-confidence which enabled her to launch herself forward without inhibition into her campaigns of pushing marriage—yet to do it with charm, to leave behind her a sense of exciting communication, of admiration for her boldness and her adventurousness.

If she had lacked this self-confidence, her approach would have been irritating; it would have been disorganized, or lacked friendliness. It might have even antagonized people.

But she had this great inner force with which she propelled herself forward toward her goals.

Wherever she went, I'm sure that she made friends.

Friends holding hands around the globe.

Samuel Johnson once wrote that "Self-confidence is the first great requisite to great undertakings."

In the words of Ralph Waldo Emerson, the great American Transcendentalist writer, "Self-trust is the first secret of success."

The Roman poet Virgil put it this way: "Let every man's hope be in himself."

Confidence, an instant confidence that wells and swells within you when you need it, this must be your great inner force.

This inner power is a quality which we all possess—to one degree or other.

It is in all of us because we have all known some successes in life—no matter how small, no matter how humble, no matter how trivial in the eyes of others.

These successes are the base upon which you can build your inner strength; you must learn to emphasize in your mind these better moments of yours, to see them in your mind, to feel them in your heart, until they become part of what you are as a breathing, living, thinking, seeing human being.

Over and over and over and over—because this is not a simple, automatic process if you have many failures to cope with, too, in your life—you must picture these good moments in your mind. You must remember you came into this world to succeed, not fail!

Over and over and over and over, you must manufacture for yourself your most successful product, your force for success. You must understand that there is good within you, forgive your faults, and rise above the blunders in your life to your triumphs of self-assertion and achievement.

It is no overnight undertaking but, in terms of days and weeks and months and years, you can enlarge in your mind this successful image of yourself, supplemented with new, rich experiences, until you have within you a great, shiny weapon—instant confidence.

Carving Your Strong Self-Image

There's a story about the great Michelangelo. Working in a stone quarry in Italy, the great sculptor was overjoyed at the sight of a huge, oblong block of stone.

He touched it. Within it he saw the spirit of Moses.

After many, many hours of working on the stone, chipping it, shaping it, he brought forth his great work of art, his great creation—of Moses and the Ten Commandments.

Now may I ask you to be your own sculptors—your tools compassion and understanding—so that you can see in your mind's eye the best that is in you, as Michelangelo pictured Moses, so that you can work to make and keep this image a reality.

For it is your self-image, which, more than anything, can guide you to years of dynamic living. If you give yourself acceptance, if you see your successes and try to perpetuate them, life will hold no great fears for you, and you will remain in the mainstream of life, doing, feeling, relating, connecting.

I offer you the Ten Commandments for creative living:
C-O-N-F-I-D-E-N-C-E:

1. C: *C*oncentrate on a stronger self-image.
2. O: *O*ffer it full partnership in your life.
3. N: *N*ever let it disappear; you must work to reinforce your sense of self.
4. F: *F*ulfill yourself with your self-image; it is your best friend.
5. I: *I*nfuse your self-image with compassion when you meet setbacks.
6. D: *D*evelop it every day; only your true sense of self can make you strong.
7. E: *E*levate yourself with your self-image so that you need not fear competition.
8. N: *N*ourish it; don't let a false sense of selflessness convince you that it is not basic to your happiness.
9. C: *C*reate a climate in which it can grow; spend time every day thinking, with humility, about yourself and your world.
10. E: *E*njoy it; continually reactivate the success instincts, the success mechanism, within you.

Remember this: Only you, with the image you build of yourself, in your mind, and which you carry with you into life, in your mind, can create giving relationships with people, productive relationships in the world of work and of interests, which can make your years bubble with life.

Confidence implies forgiveness. You feel too big to be threatened, too self-reliant, too nimble at relaxing away emotional hurts. So you are able to forgive.

You forgive others with no strings attached—a clean slate, no vestige of condemnation. A difficult task, but you can do it.

And you forgive yourself as you forgive others.

For forgiveness is but another reflection of confidence—instant confidence.

Exercise 8

Make yourself comfortable each day you work on this exercise, sitting or lying down in a quiet place where you can concentrate.

It is evening, your day is ending, but tomorrow is another day. Tomorrow will be a good day; you will do everything you can to make it a good day.

What is it you wish for tomorrow? What goal are you setting for yourself, and what can you do to attain it?

Prepare yourself for it. Close your eyes and see yourself moving toward it; help propel yourself toward it, gearing your success mechanism, oiling its hinges so it will function for you.

Let me give you a specific example:

You are an insurance salesman; you're getting by, but you're not setting the world on fire. Your goal is to make a good sale tomorrow, a happy sale, one which will contribute to the well-being of your client and earn you a healthy commission, too.

You have only one appointment in the morning, but two in the afternoon—and one is a good prospect, X. X. is a department store executive; you've seen him once, talked to him briefly, and left some materials for him to read. You've sized up his situation and feel you know the policy that will fit in with his needs. Then what's the trouble?

You see the scene in your mind. X. has a large private office on the second floor of the department store; he is an important executive and, when you saw him the first time, he was constantly interrupted—phone calls, buzzers, secretary popping in and out. You felt the efficiency of his life-wire functioning.

And you felt inferior to him. You had something good to sell him, you were thinking of his interests as well as your own, *but why should he buy from someone as worthless as you?* You fear your eyes will be shifty, your manner apologetic.

This is what's blocking your chief goal for tomorrow: your feeling about yourself.

Now let's see what we can do about it, and this time let's

bring all the exercises in this book into play. Get up and look at yourself in the mirror, with friendly eyes; see that you are human and give yourself a chance. Bring out your negative beliefs about yourself, and work to chip them down to reasonable dimensions. Sit down, comfortably, close your eyes again, and remember a good sale you made—you've had a few sales in the midst of your failures. Visualize it, the way you felt, the way you talked, bring the feel of it back into your blood, into your bones. See it over and over and over.

Then visualize a second sale you made, and keep it alive in your mind. Keep alive the feeling of your successes.

Over and over and over. And over.

Maybe you'll reach your goal tomorrow with the department store executive. But, if you don't, there's always the next day—and the next.

Chances are you will reach your goals if you keep working at what you need—instant confidence.

Whether you are an insurance salesman, doing this exercise, or a housewife, setting up an appropriate goal, or a teacher, preparing for tomorrow's objectives in the classroom, this is what you must build, with hard work and unceasing determination, stone by stone—instant confidence.

Instant Confidence and Creative Living

All right, you've read this chapter.

You see the importance of confidence—of the inner force which I call instant confidence.

You understand its relation to the success mechanism, its relation to the strength of your self-image, and you see that it is a vital factor in the life of any human being who strives for goals and successes and self-satisfaction.

Many factors may help you in life—money, position, physical constitution, good fortune. Sunshine, ocean air may refresh you; friends may bolster you.

Still, your style of living depends on you, on your inner strength—or your inner weakness.

The right setting may be pleasant.

But it is not basic.

Your inner force, this is *basic* to creative living.

You cannot start too soon to work on the emotional powers within you.

If you are twenty-one, it is not too soon.

If you are twelve, it is not too soon.

If you are twelve months old, it is not too soon.

At the same time, if you are forty-five, you are not too old. And, if you are sixty-five, you are not too old.

You must dig within yourself for your inner wealth. You must work dedicatedly, in your own interests, to put in the spotlight of your mind the successes in your life. It may be hard work, but it is worth it.

This is the key that opens the way to successful experiences in your world.

To creative living.

Instant confidence.

• 10 •

Instant Frustration:
That Inner Destructive Force

My FRIEND Salvadore Dali, the world-renowned Spanish artist, a student of psycho-cybernetics and self-image psychology, presented me with a painting depicting his concept of self-image psychology. The canvas had a world in its center. On one side, half the world was in shadow; the other half was in sunlight. Half the world in shadow to the left revealed a shrunken image; a midget walking away from the world in the black tunnels of despair toward the black angel of destruction waiting for him. To the right was the world of sunlight: man's self-image was very tall, walking toward the dawn of accomplishment with a swallow flying toward the sun.

To the left, in the world of darkness, was a man on a ship about to be capsized, floundering on rough seas of negative feelings. To the right, in the world of sunlight, the man was in a ship moving in calm waters toward port, toward a goal; peace of mind. Thus, on a canvas sixteen by fourteen inches, Dali painted his concept of the two worlds of each of us: half the world in darkness from frustration; half the world in sunlight through confidence.

It is like this when our astronauts fly around the world in their capsule at the speed of seventeen hundred five hundred miles an hour to discover the treasures of outer space: half the world is in darkness, half in sunlight.

Astronaut White took a walk outside his capsule for about twenty minutes. Suppose you walk with me for twenty minutes in the spaces of your mind as we look at the world of frustration. The world of instant frustration.

Instant confidence, instant frustration—two conflicting forces within us, continually at war with each other: the will for achievement, the will for self-destruction. You must see this world of frustration within you so that you can overcome it.

These are the distorted, dark faces of F-R-U-S-T-R-A-T-I-O-N.

1. F: *Fear.*
2. R: *Retreat.*
3. U: *Unconditional* surrender (of your self-image).
4. S: *Seeking* excuses.
5. T: *Traitor* to yourself.
6. R: *Resignation.*
7. A: *Agitation.*
8. T: *Termites* of nothingness.
9. I: *Inadequacy.*
10. O: *Oppression.*
11. N: *Negative* feelings.

They spell out an enforced retreat from the world, from yourself, into your own concentration camp of futility.

1. *Fear.* This is an important aspect of frustration. What is fear, and how does it rise? We come into the world in uncertainty, we live in uncertainty, and we pass on in uncertainty. All this creates fear. But the business of living is

to stand up under stress, to bend uncertainty to our will, and, by reactivating the success mechanism within us, to reach self-fulfillment. We come into the world to succeed, not to fail! In confidence, you see on the motion picture screen of your mind moments of pleasure most of the time, moments that may not have happened yet, which implies that you are *trying, trying* to succeed. In fear you see in your mind unhappy moments mostly, often before they have happened, because you are *trying, trying* to fail in your undertaking. And you do fail simply because you can't think creatively with negative feelings any more than you can think destructively with positive feelings.

No one is immune from fear; the happiest human beings experience fear now and then. The important thing is to recognize that fear, like confidence, can be an emotional carry-over from one day to the next when you make a chronic habit of it. *Chronic* fear, not fear, is your enemy. Fear day in and day out creates a destructive climate of *existing,* not living, contributing to a state of instant frustration.

You must not mistake excitement for fear. Creative excitement implies confidence: you have a goal in mind and you will not permit anything, any failure or fear, to stand in the way of achieving this goal. Destructive excitement, when there is *no goal* in mind, involves fear. It is important to decide what you want to do, not what you don't want to do. For example, suppose there are five ways of reaching a goal and you are uncertain which road to take. Here anxiety (fear) is productive because you have a goal in mind. You use anxiety creatively to decide which of the five roads you will take, and once you make up your mind you proceed toward your destination. If you fail, you try again the next day and the next until you succeed. Success means rising above fear.

2. *Retreat.* A basic ingredient of instant frustration is retreat; it can be thrust upon you, or you can thrust it upon yourself. You move away from life, from yourself, in a withdrawal which is in conflict with your success instincts.

An occasional, "strategic" retreat can be helpful—as when one withdraws into his mind for a short period of time each day to regain his peace of mind and renew his spiritual energies for the everyday battles of life.

A basic retreat is something else; there is only self-destruction in it. The person who chronically spends his time alone, "resting," or "lying down," is succumbing to a most unfortunate form of self-negation.

John Locke, the English thinker, a man of rare common sense, once wrote that "Men's happiness or misery is for the most part of their own making."

This is obviously true. *Only you can force yourself to retreat into misery and self-pity.*

Retreat is frustrating because it is a movement away from natural life forces. You must learn to cope with your negative feelings *now,* to activate your successful instincts *now.*

3. *Unconditional surrender* (of your self-image). Once you are the victim of chronic frustration, you surrender your self-image, your feeling of worth. You feel as if you are a vacuum, an empty shell impersonating a human being; it is obvious that you will feel an inner apathy, a sense of "what's the use—there's nothing in life for me."

The person who surrenders unconditionally has lost all hope. He has given up on himself completely; he is living out his days with no other purpose but to survive. Feeling as if he is of no value, he just goes through the motions and thinks of ways to "pass the time."

But we all have good in us; we have all had some successes, no matter how small. Almost everyone has, no matter how short and sad the duration, known what it is to feel and to receive the healing miracle of love.

Friedrich Wilhelm Froebel, who made such outstanding contributions to educational theory, once wrote in *The Education of Man*: "A suppressed or perverted good quality—a good tendency, only repressed, misunderstood, or misguided—lies originally at the bottom of every shortcoming in man. Hence the only and infallible remedy for counteracting any shortcomings and even wickedness is to find the original good source, the originally good side of the human being that has been repressed, distributed, or misled into the shortcoming, and then to foster, build up, and properly guide this good side. Thus, the shortcoming will at last disappear, although it may involve a hard struggle *against habit but not against original depravity* in man, and this is accomplished so much the more rapidly and surely because man himself tends to abandon his shortcomings, for man prefers right to wrong."

Your task is to find this "original good source" in yourself.

Once you consistently see yourself as "good," you will not retreat from life, resort to evasions, eat yourself up with termites of nothingness.

You will not feel inner apathy. And you will not surrender your sense of self.

4. *Seeking excuses.* Another aspect of instant frustration is seeking excuses for an error, rather than admitting it and rising above it. Seeking excuses involves avoiding goal attainment; rising above an error is a goal in itself. When one avoids setting worthwhile goals, one day is as dull as the next. This encourages one to do nothing, to leave things until tomorrow. *Mañana* is a Spanish word meaning "tomorrow," and members of Mañana Incorporated often really mean "never."

The excuse-seeking of *mañana* constitutes one of the faces of frustration because the "tomorrow" philosophy leads to the living of goal-less days. One becomes passive, retreating from life's responsibilities into negligent attitudes.

Mañana Incorporated is a huge international organization; everywhere there are people who put things off until "tomorrow."

The *mañana* philosophy is frustrating because it is based on illusion: that a wonderful tomorrow will come when goals will be easier to accomplish, when problems will be easier to solve, when blocks will disappear and there will be no frustrations.

When this wonderful day comes, then the millions of members of Mañana Incorporated will go to work and get things done.

But this day will not come.

At least I know that I won't live to see it. And neither will you.

So the *mañana* philosophy is merely wishful thinking, a

fantasy, and it leads to retreat, to resignation—to all the other aspects of frustration.

The destructive *mañana* philosophy is quite different from the New Nostalgia, which is a longing to improve oneself today and tomorrow. One is passive, the other active. One should always look ahead to improve oneself; that goes without saying.

Get out of the *mañana* habit. Whenever you can, and your goals are worthwhile, do them today. This will keep you going, doing, and this is good for you.

5. *Traitor to yourself*. This is another facet of frustration.

The word "traitor" may sound extreme, but it isn't. When you lead yourself into an unproductive pattern of living, you are being a traitor to yourself, to your promise of self-realization, to your responsibility to society.

You will be a traitor to yourself—

  if you do not set goals for yourself each day

  if you do not take an active interest in doing things

  if you do not encourage your creative curiosity

  if you do not go toward the world with vigor

  if you do not reactivate your success mechanism and work to strengthen your self-image.

You will, instead, enmesh yourself in negative feelings and more negative feelings, a cycle which leads to instant frustration.

6. *Resignation*. This is closely allied to the other feelings and feeling-actions I've already described and is part of the instant frustration syndrome.

It involves renunciation—of the world of people and of yourself.

It is a form of "unconditional surrender," but when the Allied leaders of World War II used this phrase, they did not mean to imply that enemy war leaders (except war criminals) should completely destroy themselves.

In our meaning of resignation, "unconditional surrender," however, is total self-destruction.

When traveling, you may wish to temporarily dispose of your luggage as you check it in a locker—but you return to claim it. You don't throw it away.

Not so with the feeling of resignation, the feeling of accepting defeat. You've given up on yourself; you refuse to call for your "luggage." You've stopped fighting for your rights. You've given up on the competition that is part of life.

This is inconsistent with the business of being alive. You must compete with yourself every day whether you like it or not; you must fight the negative feelings inside you. You cannot straddle the fence; you must make a decision. You must jump on one side or the other: toward life or away from life; toward strengthening your awareness and acceptance of yourself or toward a childish relapse into impotence.

You can resign from a job; you can resign from a club; you can walk away from friends who annoy you. But you cannot resign from your basic membership in the human family—or from your self-image. To do so is suicide.

7. *Agitation.* Agitation, usually born of unproductive resentment, leads to elimination.

In a footrace a contestant may be disqualified for one reason or another; it is up to the judges. But in the daily race for survival, only we can disqualify ourselves. But, when we do, the race still goes on, and it is a marathon—in our minds. In our minds we run around and around the track, frustrated, never stopping, thoughts staggering—until we fall apart, exhausted, with nothing to show for it but irritation and loneliness.

Why run an agitated "Mad Hatter, Alice-in-Wonderland" race in our minds? We must walk, not run, into the world of activity, into competition with others (with cooperation, too), toward our usefulness as people. We walk erect to the full stature of our self-respect. We walk, calm and collected, with no tension but with confidence, and think of what we can offer the crowd—of what we can offer ourselves. We walk without twitching, without cracking our knuckles in agitation.

We return to ourselves, to the strengthening of our self-image, to a daily life of self-renewal, self-improvement, self-atonement for our poor judgment in wasting time on past mistakes. We walk erect, proud of our self-image, an image in God's Image.

8. *Termites of nothingness.* Termites eat wood; they destroy products of human ingenuity, and people therefore think of them with dismay.

Therefore, when I refer to "termites of nothingness" as a face of instant frustration, it is because this is a process of eating into yourself in a self-destructive manner—until there remains nothingness in feeling.

In withdrawing from life, you eat into yourself, smashing your spirit. Like an injured man suffering from loss of blood, passive living drains away your spiritual "blood," casting off your vitality.

A doctor puts a cast on a fractured leg to limit motion and accelerate healing. The patient use crutches to take the pressure from his broken leg; until it heals, he must limit his mobility.

But this is creative planning—and the end result should be the restoration of the leg to health and of the person to full functioning in life.

A man who suffers from chronic frustration uncreatively eats into his mind until he fractures it; then he puts a cast on it, deliberately limiting his life activities.

He rationalizes what he has done. He blames his poor communication with others on others, feels that he is misunderstood, complains about the injustice of humanity, and limits his efforts in communicating with other people—until he ends up communicating only with himself. Sitting, brooding, suffering.

Do you recall the story of Mr. R.? An "African bug" ate its way into this fine man's mind, and he withdrew from the generous, outgoing maturity which characterized him into a frightened, self-destructive shell. Once helped to rid himself of the emotional termites in his mind, he was able to recover his confidence in himself and go back into the world, where he was a constructive member of society.

We all have our "African bugs," small and large, operating in our minds in many different ways because of the diabolical complexity of our world. We must not let them eat into us, forcing our withdrawal from other people.

To live creatively, you must continue to play ball, to communicate in the world—no matter what your problems. Otherwise your hibernation will produce a media in which termites of nothingness will multiply. They will bore into your self-image, crushing it until you feel like a passive doormat.

Stop this self-flagellation! Learn to *cybernate,* not hibernate!

9. *Inadequacy.* Frustration indicates inadequacy, which activates a retreat from life; when this happens, you are guilty of a painful sidestepping. By choice you avoid people and the realities of the world, the pains and the sorrows, and in this evasion you deprive yourself of all life's treasures.

Your avoidance of life might seem necessary to you; you might tell yourself that you are unlucky or that other people are inconsiderate and cruel, that they dislike you.

There might be *some* truth in the ideas with which you avoid genuine human relationships—but there is almost always another side to the coin.

Evasion of one's role as a human being among people is a pit of despair.

Do you remember the story of Mickey? He was a very young man, but he withdrew from life—pain, depression, evasion—days of turning his back on people and on himself, sleepwalking into an inner critical, hostile loneliness which sweltered like a waterless desert inside him.

Until Mickey found an oasis, found it in a turning toward a girl. In giving of himself, in giving her his compassion, he fought his way back into the world of meaning—from inadequacy to a true sense of self.

10. *Oppression.* This is yet another face of instant frustration in which you take away the oxygen from your mental lungs; continually short of breath, you exist, you do not live. Fearful, you lack enthusiasm for living; feeling persecuted, you relapse into a state of boredom. Nothing is exciting for the oppressed person; no goal means anything at all. The oppressed person blocks his own positive feelings, feels instead a weariness of mind and body. He is always bored.

You will find boredom among people of all ages, even youngsters in their teens—any parent, for that matter, knows that little children of two or three can be bored—if they have no basic respect for their movement-toward-life drive.

Yet there is so much excitement in living in the world.

Michel de Montaigne, the sixteenth-century French philosopher, once wrote in "Of the Education of Children": "This great world, which some do yet multiply as several species under one genus, is the mirror wherein we are to behold ourselves, to be able to know ourselves as we ought to do in the true bias. . . . So many humors, so many sects, so many judgments, opinions, laws, and customs teach us to judge aright of our own and inform our understanding to discover its imperfection and natural infirmity. . . . So many mutations of state and kingdoms and so many turns and revolutions of public fortune will make us wise enough to make no great wonder of our own. . . ."

Montaigne is writing about knowing yourself, of course, but the thing I *feel* in this passage is his communication of the many-sided excitement of life; he sees and feels life in all its exciting complexity. Reading this, one feels that this man would not have been bored if he had lived to be three hundred for his mind is alive with action and thought, complexity and possibility.

The oppressed person, however, will not allow himself to feel this excitement; if he does, he insists on destroying it in himself.

Let us assume that each day you take a bath. When you are through bathing, you pull the lever and the water escapes through the drainhole in the bathtub. Soon the tub is empty.

Use your imagination further now; think of boredom as a process in which, instead of water, it is your precious feelings which flow out of you into the bathtub and down the drainhole, leaving you empty, a wreck of a human being. All that is left for you is—boredom.

If you think of oppression, or boredom, in this way, you will protect your capacity to enjoy life: by filling yourself with images of your past successes, by forgiving yourself for your mistakes, by fortifying in yourself the vital fluids of your self-image.

And you will not let your strength flow out of you and down the drain.

11. *Negative feelings*. We lay great stress these days on our crippling physical diseases, and rightly so. But negative feelings are the greatest killers of people—while they live —the killers of their souls. And frustration is bound up in negativism.

Millions of people nurse negative feelings: "I'm too young to do anything"; "Middle age is boring"; "I'm old, so I'm useless"; "No one wants me for anything"; "The world's no good; who would bring a child into this world?"

This kind of thinking must go, or there can be no creative living. Anyone planning creative years must wipe out this kind of thinking, or he will defeat himself and know frustration all his life.

In the United States today increasing attention is being directed toward education and toward the implementation of President Lyndon Johnson's "Great Society"—and this is fine—but we must also reeducate people to plan, without negative attitudes, toward fulfilling years.

Your Precious Hours

These, then, are the ingredients of instant frustration, and you must avoid its traps as avidly as you would try to avoid a politician who promises to *raise* taxes.

In the previous chapter I mentioned what instant confidence really is—revisualizing, reemphasizing the winning moments that create in us an ongoing productive drive. Revisualizing, reemphasizing your losing feelings, so that they become habits, leads to instant frustration.

Instant confidence, instant frustration. Which shall it be?

You have many, many years. You have many, many days—to live, to enjoy.

And many, many, many hours. Precious hours.

You must learn who you are and what you are doing to yourself. You must learn to enjoy these hours of these days. You must learn to enjoy each little thing you do, to concentrate on what is meaningful for you.

You must learn that you are somebody important, a person who puts together the best there is in you and uses it—connectedly.

In your precious years.

In your precious days.

In your precious hours.

Exercise 9

Every now and then, for a few seconds, you sit down and close your eyes. In the motion picture theater of your mind today, you will see a double feature: on the screen will be two motion pictures of yourself.

In the first, you are in a sailboat about to capsize. The wind tosses the boat about like paper and has ripped off the sails. The wind is blowing your boat away from the shore, and your chances of survival are slim; you cling to some wood, but you have no hope. You say to yourself: "I've put myself in this untenable position by concentrating on my failures in life. Now there is nothing but frustration. I have no one to blame but myself!"

Now the picture changes. You see the second motion picture of yourself. You are in a sailboat gliding toward the docks in calm waters. You feel sunburned and healthy; the sun shines down on you. You say to yourself: "I've put myself in this wonderful position by turning my back on negative feelings and concentrating on the confidence of past successes. I feel instant confidence. I have goals and I will reach them."

Your world within you is divided into two parts: one half in shadow from frustration, the other half in sunlight from confidence. You say to yourself, "I resolve to renew my confidence every day—until it is second nature to me. I shall rise above obstacles. I shall succeed because I was born to succeed!"

This exercise has no value at all if you merely see these two pictures of yourself and merely talk about what you are planning to do.

You must *feel* and *do*. Lip service is not enough.

You must *feel* that you are in those two boats and are

living these scenes. You must *feel* the drastic difference between the two situations. When Sir Laurence Olivier acts as if he were Hamlet, he *believes* he is Hamlet, and you believe it, too.

You must act out your part, too, emphasizing the positive picture of you, the one in which you have renounced the capsized ship of frustration and are sailing in a durable ship of confidence, certain that you will reach port.

Soon you will discard the negative picture. You will see only the happy picture of your arrival in port. You must *try, try* every day to reach your confident feelings for the very act of trying releases you from frustration and propels you toward your full stature of self-respect.

Don't be cynical about the exercises in this book; don't doubt the power of your mind. Instead, see if they won't help you; do them, and see if they won't help you.

Do this exercise as often as you can. It may help you to get on your feet, reactivating the success mechanism within you.

• 11 •

Living with Your
Emotional Scars

LIFE *is* scars.

There is no life without emotional scars; no one escapes unblemished, no one can claim perfection without perpetrating a mockery upon himself.

Jesus, the great example of humility for mankind, said, "Let him who hast not sinned cast the first stone."

We have all sinned; we are all scarred.

In my life there have always been *physical* scars. As a kid, I was a member of a tough gang of New York boys; our days were full of knee-skinning and elbow-scraping—the more, the better—and we wore our physical scars as medals of distinction. We had this in common with millions of kids everywhere—in Chicago, Los Angeles, London, Moscow—and everywhere there are kids who run and shout and skin their knees.

As an adult, as a plastic surgeon, my connection with physical scars has been more unique. With operations, with the successful remodeling of people's physical appearance go scar formation. They are part of the process of healing.

Still all these physical scars are benign. The damage is superficial—there is, in fact, no real damage at all.

But, as I grew older and wiser, I saw in people—sometimes in myself—signs of inner distress. So much suffering, hurt feelings, confusion, guilt, so many people holding grudges, submerged with bitterness, feeling inferior and worthless. I thought of these as scars, as emotional scars.

But these emotional scars, I came to see, were so much deeper than physical scars, so much more painful.

You people who have bought this book, who read my words and think about them, so many of you are emotionally scarred. You carry these scars with you into your teen-age and adult years. These scars in most instances stem from seeing yourself at your worst instead of at your best or else from keeping up with someone else's image instead of your own; for example, an unhappy home life, loss of a sweetheart or loved one, an unhappy marriage, loss of a job—any one of which may not be your fault. But, what can you do about them?

You cannot avoid the scars; there is no escape from mistakes, quarrels, and misunderstandings to which human beings are prey.

We have all erred in our individual ways; how do we live with our errors?

There is a clue in the Bible. "When I was a child, I spake as a child, I understood as a child, I thought as a child; but when I became a man, I put away childish things."

The answer lies in treating your emotional scars from a mature point of view. You cannot adopt a child's approach and ask for magic that will make all troubles and grievances disappear. You must handle them maturely.

You Must Face Up to Life

To begin with, you must acknowledge the realities in our world. Only a person who blinds himself sees perfection in it; the thinking, feeling person sees complexity. He refuses to gain an uneasy peace of mind with self-deluding denials of reality.

It's eleven o'clock; time for the news. On goes your television set. A man comes to life, hair slicked back, white shirt, neat suit, polished manner. "Twenty-five above-ground nuclear explosions today . . . scientists warn of seven hundred percent increase in life-destroying radioactivity in the air. . . . Five new nations have exploded atomic bombs this week. . . . X threatens war over the X dispute; world war looms. . . . X declares the XYZ war will go on another five years, with geometrically increasing casualties, total casualties ten million. . . ."

Thank God, a commercial. A sweet-looking young lady threatens you with various diseases for a minute or so.

Back to the news. "Civil rights rioting in the North, East, West, and South. . . . Water shortage all over the U.S.; all water taps will be turned off from noon to 5 P.M. . . . Internal Revenue catches one million tax evaders, sentenced to hanging at dawn. . . . The weather; seven straight days of fog, no planes can take off. . . .

Does this sound familiar? *Certainly not; news reports like this, and none of us could long survive.* No one would ever turn on the news, either. We would pick up our TV sets and heave them out of windows.

But, in truth, there *is* much uncertainty and danger in the world—just as we, as individuals, face much uncertainty and danger in our own lives. It is our responsibility, our commitment to our self-respect to overcome emotional problems and upsetting experiences. We cannot stick our heads in the sand or in the clouds; we cannot run away from life's scarring, past, present, or future.

Now, then, do we live with it? How do we face up to reality without letting reality crush us?

First, go back to the end of Chapter 5 and reread the story about the little baby in Nicaragua, whose harelip tore apart two loving families. And read Exercise 4 again in that same chapter. Then, here's some emotional "penicillin" for you, and you don't need a prescription. The first is a new way of finding peace and relaxation in this uncertain world of ours. The second two are our faithful friends, forgiveness and a strong self-image. Remember the image of the man on the bicycle going forward. If he falls off the bike, he gets back on in order to reach his destination. Here's how you can do just that:

1. Escape now and then.
2. Learn to forgive.
3. Strengthen your reluctant self-image.

First, let's talk about escaping from your problems and tensions so that you can defeat them.

When I talk about escape, I don't mean a permanent retreat from the world of problems; I mean a temporary interval of peace, in which one can think about things without fear and bring back the heart and body of his soul to face life's struggles, feeling renewed.

Here's a fascinating story; read it.

An Escape into Self-Discovery

Twenty years ago, after delivering some lectures in Italy, I decided to travel around for a few days. I heard about the beauty of Ischia, and boarded the boat to its shores.

Ischia, on the Mediterranean, is breathtaking to see. As you approach it in the early morning mist, this island seems enchanted: its black stone foundations are invisible, and you see only parapets and castle towers, which the sunlight bathes a gorgeous pink.

Then the mists clear. You see a small island town—not a fairy castle—with burghers' houses, cathedral, market square, and a massive citadel stretching overhead. Blue sea, blue skies! As you come closer still, you feel swallowed up in silence—and then you sense an incredible thing about the little island town.

No interested faces stare down at you; the market square is a vacuum; only the cries of the gulls break the quiet. High on rock, deep in rock, Ischia slumbers in the sunlight, and once more you feel under the spell of the ages—a prisoner in an eternal fairy tale.

Twenty years before, Ischia was deserted, had been deserted for many, many years.

Once there had been thousands of people. Then followed centuries of siege and countersiege, with French, Italian, and Spanish princes in turn holding the citadel; the end came in installments. The townspeople drifted to the mainland; by 1790 less than a hundred were left. Soon they left, too.

A tunnel carved out of rock leads you upward. The sunlight fades behind and memories of the past seem to whisper around you—the Crusaders who paused en route to the Holy Land, the feudal lords, the Barbary corsairs, gone now. . . .

Around a curve of the tunnel, you find a shrine to the Virgin. In front of the shrine burns a candle.

I turned to my guide, puzzled. "If Ischia is deserted, who lit the candle?"

"It's not entirely deserted, sir. One man stays; we will talk to him."

We resumed our climb. The tunnel curved again, sunlight burst upon us, and we found ourselves in the center of town. There was the cathedral, roofless. A lizard slithered over the dusty pavement; the gulls cried out.

"Here," said my guide, from a parapet. "This is fascinating, sir."

There was a terrifying drop below where he stood, on rock, hundreds of feet down to the sea. Boulders on the beach below seemed pebbles. "This was where they used to bring criminals, captured enemies—in the old days," said my guide. "They would tie them up, leave them to meditate on their crimes. Then the executioners would come. A push, a scream—falling, falling." He looked down. "Terrible way to die!"

For awhile I had been expecting to hear a voice. "Where is the fellow who lives alone on this island?" I asked.

"In the bishop's palace."

Crossing the square, we threaded through an alley, entered the palace courtyard.

Within the palace you could look up through gaps in the

vaulted roof and see blue sky, dazzling sun. Below were
the walls of the island citadel, plunging down to the sunny
sea, stretching for miles and miles, winking and glistening
until it merged with the horizon. At the horizon was a blur,
smoke-soft—Italy.

"Welcome," a voice said.

I had expected a wrinkled old man, but the hermit of
Ischia was young. He had dark eyes and curly hair; he
wore a peasant's shirt and trousers and heavy leather
sandals.

"Please, help yourselves," he said, pointing to bread and
cheese. But we had taken our own, with sausage and a
flask of wine.

When we had finished eating, he filled a basin and gravely
offered it to us. He tossed the water out the window; it
shattered in sunlight and seemed to fall a thousand miles.

Then he sat back, calmly, and looked at us.

"The view must make up for a lot," I said.

"Make up for what?"

"The solitude."

"Ah," he smiled. "The solitude. I was aware of it when
first I came to Ischia . . ."

"When was that?"

"I have no calendar; perhaps seven or eight months."

"Why did you take up this solitary life?"

His cat was stretched out on the window ledge, his only
companion in the huge castle.

"There's nothing mysterious. Just boredom."

"You're a fine-looking young man," I observed. "You
must have had friends."

He paused, looking directly into my eyes, obviously won-
dering if he should speak frankly or end our conversation.
He decided to talk.

"Yes, I had friends," he said, "and I was thought fortunate. My parents were wealthy, influential; with no effort,
I could have almost any position I chose. My marriage
had been arranged to an attractive, wealthy girl, and I liked
her all right. . . . But I was bored.

"I discovered this one evening while dressing for a party.

Pretty girls would be there. I had a boat in the harbor; later I would suggest a moonlight sail.

"I was brushing my hair when, suddenly, everything seemed dull. Not just the party, but my whole life.

"At the party, the prettiest girl liked me. When I suggested a moonlight sail, she agreed; soon we were on the Bay of Naples. I was steering the boat and embracing the girl, who was affectionate. What more could I ask?

"Still, I felt overwhelmed with boredom. The girl, sensing my feeling, asked me to take her home; I didn't care. I just wanted to go to just one place—to Ischia.

"In the morning I asked myself 'Why Ischia?' I hadn't thought of the deserted little town on the island since my father had taken me years before.

"I couldn't forget Ischia. Finally, I set out to see it again.

"Ischia's shores were beautiful. I jumped out of the boat, climbed up through the tunnel to the square below. Suddenly my depression was gone.

"I didn't understand why, but I gave thanks. By nightfall I was tired, but in fine spirits. Ischia looks different at night; the towers, walls, parapets shimmer into fascinating patterns—like a beautiful painting in the moonlight. An El Greco, perhaps.

"I did not sleep that night. Toward dawn I half-awoke, almost in a trance. Suddenly I really saw myself—through the eyes of others. I knew why I had been so desolate, why an impulse had propelled me to Ischia.

"My boredom had come from surrendering to every appetite. No interest remained.

"Finally I recalled a happy day; I was a boy and my father had taken me to Ischia. I had been happy that day, alive, curious to see the world. Now, yearning for that wonderful feeling of long ago, I had returned as a man.

"That first day I was once more the adventuring youth; my spirits had bubbled when I stepped on Ischia's shores. But the illusion would fade; then what? Was there only a return to my old world, where I had everything but felt I had nothing?

"I considered the two extremes: the city, with its crowds,

its noise, its battles, its sensual delights: Ischia, the deserted
island town. Here, if I was to find interest in life, I would
have to create it in myself. If I could, maybe I could then
create pleasure for myself in my real world.

"Could I test my idea? I resolved to try, for a year. . . .

"Now my year is about up . . . I do not want to return,
but I am ready."

His eyes seemed to come back to the present. "I have
found a precious spirit inside myself," he said.

"Few people could afford to go to an Ischia for almost
a year," I said.

"I am fortunate," he said. "I have learned what I had
to, and will not need Ischia again. But you can make an
Ischia anywhere: a quiet room to retreat to, alone, for the
exploration of your spirit."

An Ischia in Your Mind

There is great meaning in this story.

Not literally—

Because few of us could financially afford such an undertaking, because a year of being alone would doubtless be
beyond our tolerance, because it would, for many of us, constitute an escape from life in a negative sense—as an evasion
of responsibility.

I ask you, therefore, to look at the lesson of this story not
literally, but in a symbolic sense.

The lesson is that sometimes life's problems are too
great; one may feel boredom and depression, as this young
man did, or tension and rage.

At such a time a temporary escape may help you lick
your wounds and heal your scars; an escape from people,
pressures, decisions to a place of quiet where you can think
things over, without interruption, without responsibilities im-
pinging.

You don't need to escape for a year; in its literal sense, as
I've indicated, this would represent a self-destructive running
away from life for most people. A day or two now and then
may help you; some days just a half hour—even less—will
do fine.

You don't need an exotic, faraway place like Ischia to go to; a quiet room in your own home is most suitable, or a pleasant place in your neighborhood, where you can feel comfortable and secure—and think about your days and your goals, where you are going and what you are doing, what your purpose is in life, and how you can build richer meaning in life for yourself and your loved ones.

For a meaningful escape from life's problems, you must also find another room: in your own mind. A room in your mind where you can think peacefully, plan sensible resolves, refresh your energies.

An Ischia in your mind!

To go to when you feel overburdened with care.

A *temporary* retreat, not an eternal hiding place from life; an aid to more creative living, not a life-death.

Then, renewed, back to the world with all its imperfections. Because it's fun.

The Joy in an Active Life

I have stressed, in the pages of this book, the joy one will feel in living an active life. I have criticized the concept of passive living.

Therefore, I must reaffirm this now so that readers will not misinterpret what I'm saying: *There is joy in the active life for all of one's life.* A goal every day, something to move toward in this pulsating world; it is terrible to throw away your years sitting around, moping, feeling sorry for yourself.

The idea of escaping into your mind now and then when you need it—and I believe most people do—is not at all inconsistent with this active philosophy of doing, moving, acting.

I must repeat that I do not recommend for many people an escape for a year to a deserted island; I told this story about the hermit of Ischia because it so beautifully illustrates the principle of cleansing oneself, of finding one's inner spirit, and because I found this man's story so fascinating and felt that my readers would also.

The person who lives creatively will stay in the swim of

things, will be busy and interested and involved—and will be able more easily to clear an hour or two for this worthwhile purpose.

He will be able to rebound from life's hard knocks.

Baseball player Larry Brown of the Cleveland Indians came back from a fractured skull which he suffered in a collision with another player to play ball again less than seven weeks later.

Entertainer Sammy Davis, Jr., was in the headlines a number of years ago after his crippling accident—but since then he has come on stronger than ever as one of America's most versatile performers.

Poet Robert Frost, honored on his seventy-fifth birthday a few years ago by the U.S. Senate, was at first ignored in his own country. It was in England that he had his first poems published; then he came home and started on the road to renown.

You, too, may have to rebound—many times—from troubles. To live creatively, you will have to stay with it and keep going. An occasional retreat may help you.

Then back to living.

The Sweetness of Forgiveness

Rule 2 for healing your emotional scars is: *forgiveness*.

First, you must forgive yourself. You must exonerate yourself for the unwise decisions you've made, for the foolish things you've said, for the times you've let yourself down, for the times you've let friends down. You must stop torturing yourself for your lack of wisdom when you needed it, for your cautiousness when you should have been bold, for your boldness when you should have been cautious. You must forgive the times when you've lost your temper over trifles, failed to stand up for your rights when you should have, stepped on other people's toes with your insensitive remarks, given in to the inconsiderate egotism that is so much a part of human nature. You must erase your shame over the hundreds and hundreds of gross and petty failures in your life.

For there is great sweetness in forgiveness; it is balm for

the scars of life. Without it, there is no quiet room in your mind to escape to for peace; there is only a room jangling with tension.

No one can live creatively if he cannot forgive his own blunders and imperfections. He is more likely to suffer from insomnia at night and fatigue during the day.

You must realize that you are a creature of God, part of God's' plan, that you are unique and have value as a human being.

You must understand that as a human being you are not perfect; see your successes, cherish them; see your faults, too, but forgive them.

Once you are able to forgive yourself, then perhaps you can forgive others. No matter who you are, you have been hurt unless you have lived in cellophane. But you must stop holding grudges.

Too many people waste their time obsessed with hatred for those who have hurt them; isn't it time to forgive and forget? Then you can make plans and set goals and work at the very satisfying project of making each day a life in itself, of living, driving, loving, challenging, moving each precious day of your lives.

Drink in the sweetness of forgiveness—of yourself and of others. You must forgive a parent, a friend, a loved one, for the errors in the past. Forgive the hurt they caused you. Forget it by loving in the present . . . now!

Your Reluctant Self-Image

In the final analysis, it is your basic acceptance of yourself, the strength of your self-image, that will enable you to combat the emotional scars of a lifetime.

If you see yourself at your best, if you visualize yourself in a manner that pleases you, you will be able to heal your scars and bind up your wounds—and you will not retreat from life into a permanent shell.

The trouble is that so many people see themselves not at their best, but at their worst. They seem unable to see the good in themselves, to image it. There is an exasperating reluctance of their self-image, a reluctance to change. They remain hostile to their image of themselves.

So many people lambaste themselves with criticism—worse than their most implacable enemy, the most persecuting inquisitor.

Let us imagine a courtroom scene. You are on trial; the judge is supposed to be a terror.

JUDGE: What's the matter with you? You look terrible.

YOU: I'm sorry, Your Honor, but I didn't have much time and before . . .

JUDGE: Did I give you permission to address the court?

YOU: Well, I . . .

JUDGE: You look like a criminal type all right. I know a criminal when I see one. What's the charge?

YOU: I'm sorry that I don't make a very good impression, Your Honor. I really try my best, I try very hard, as a matter of . . .

JUDGE: No apologies, they will not help you at all. Now let's get down to the facts of the case so that I can sentence you. It is obvious to me that you deserve an extremely severe penalty.

Does this ridiculous courtroom scene horrify you or does it merely make you laugh?

It should do neither because the judge persecutes you in this monstrous courtroom no more severely than many of you persecute yourselves in your minds. And you, as courtroom participant, are no more outrageously apologetic than you are to yourselves when dwelling on your shortcomings —many of you reading this book.

So many people in this world shortchange themselves; so many give themselves no chance at all to succeed—as in this ludicrous courtroom.

Further, most people's self-images are reluctant, reluctant to change. It is difficult for them to break a lifetime of habit; of seeing themselves as inferior, of criticizing themselves for this or that, of finding solace in some acceptable form of passivity or in some safe type of conformity.

If you want to live comfortably, joyfully, in spite of the emotional scarring that is part of the life process, you must do more than learn to escape and forgive—helpful as these processes are.

You must learn to see yourself as a worthwhile human being who deserves good things in life. You must build and build your self-image.

You must feel good enough about yourself so that you can enjoy your days.

You must tell yourself it is time for enjoyment.

If you feel you're worth it.

Exercise 10

All you need for this exercise, as for most of them, is a chair and a quiet room in which you can relax.

Sink back into your chair; close your eyes.

What is bothering you? What are those anxious thoughts churning through your brain, chasing each other? You may have failed that course in English? Your children are too rebellious? Not enough money coming in? Your boss criticized you? Your mother-in-law is sick?

Now try to slow down these panicky thoughts; slower, slower. Get them to slow down so you can stop their flow completely.

So that you can escape for just a little while—if only for ten minutes. If you can spare a half hour, so much the better.

Relax in your chair now, and resolve to give your mind a short vacation. Think more pleasant thoughts and reinforce them with relaxing images.

In your mind see yourself lying on the beach, the ocean waves beating against the shore, the sun bathing you in its heat. Feel the salt tang in the air; see the blue of the sky. Or see the mountains you walked over during that vacation three years ago. Picture the trees and bushes, the coolness of the air, the fun of picking berries.

Or see in your mind some incident in the past which pleased you: your boss shaking your hand in a friendly spirit; depositing some money in your savings account; asserting your point of view aggressively; walloping a golf ball high and far and watching it land. See these images; feel your pleasure in them.

Escape for awhile and enjoy it. Run out into the ocean, plunge into the waves, feel the refreshment.

When you feel better, come back to today—and forgive.

Forgive yourself for the mistakes you've made today; you're only human.

Forgive the people who hurt you today; perhaps they meant no harm. And, if they did, holding grudges will not help you. Only positive action to right the situation will help, the positive action of a person with a growing self-image.

Forgive the world for its imperfections; vow to live intensely in it and to make each day a good one. Even if something is always going wrong, even with strikes and inflation and disturbing news, you can make your day go right.

See your better side in your mental mirror. See yourself as someone who can rise above a hurt, a blunder, an emotional scar. See yourself as the calm, happy person you can be—the person you really are.

Do your scars feel just a little less painful? All right, now that you feel less sorry for yourself, think of some goals for yourself.

For now. Or, if it's late at night, for tomorrow.

It will be a good day for you. Make it a good day.

Forget yesterday.

Work toward a creative goal *now*.

Tasting the
Heady Wine of Friendship

YOU TURN the dial of your radio; it lights up and out comes music.

The music may be sweet and melodious; it may be harsh and jangling.

But, usually, one theme underlies it. The longing for love —for friendship.

The lyrics may be sensitive or trite; they may be lovely or moronic; they may be Cole Porter sophistication or unimaginative vulgarity.

Still, no matter how crude, they are verbalizations of the agonizing human need for love—for friendship.

Music is one of our primary means of communication; in our complex civilized world it is directly emotional and appeals to basic human nature.

In other communication media we find the same emphasis. In books, in magazines, we find that people hungrily seek friendship.

Often, in these money-greedy, sensation-wild days, this craving takes the form of an avid sexual curiosity—usually cheap and pornographic, sometimes genuine.

Still, if we penetrate the many disguises under which the friendship instinct operates, we come to a fundamental human need which our communication media so headline: *the need for deep friendship between people.*

It is an urgent need, one that has always been with human beings, as far back as historians can reach in their accounts of human life on this planet.

More than two thousand years ago Aristotle, the learned Greek philosopher, whose influence lasted through the Middle Ages until modern times, wrote: "What is a friend? A single soul dwelling in two bodies."

In Apocrypha: Ecclesiastes 6:16 we find: "A faithful friend is the medicine of life."

Better than medicine, really. Medicine is for those already ill; friendship is basically for the well to enjoy, a joy to keep them well throughout their lifetime.

Life without friendship is like cereal without milk; there can be no sense of completion. Real friendship is a subtle, trusting interrelationship whose worth is too great to be measured.

In the words of America's first President, George Washington, "Be courteous to all, but intimate with few, and let those few be well tried before you give them your confidence. True friendship is a plant of slow growth, and must undergo and withstand the shocks of adversity before it is entitled to the appellation." (It is interesting to note that, as with a friendship, George Washington's image has grown with time. He is no longer seen as the Godlike figure he once was or as the incompetent that others have tried to make him, but as a human being—with virtues and faults, a great cementing force in our national development.)

Another great President, Thomas Jefferson, once compared friendship to wine.

Yes, like good wine, friendship can give you a lift.

Like wine, it lasts. Inclement conditions do not destroy it.

And, as Jefferson points out, it is "restorative"; it renews a person grappling with life's problems, refreshing him so that, given a good night's sleep, he can call once again upon his resources to go toward the battles of life.

Friendship is a treasure.

It is a fundamental ingredient in the cooking pot of the delicious dish that is creative living.

The Meaning of Friendship

It is sad that many of us become disappointed in the results of friendship, that instead of enriching us they leave us wounded, causing us to think less of others and more of our-

selves. We seldom think that perhaps we have been at fault.
It usually seems to be the other person.

Friendship is giving.

In Chapter 3 we talked about how we can get more fun
out of other people by improving our relationships with
them—that we can't withdraw from life, but that we must
give our all to form satisfying relationships.

Friendship is not what we take from others but what we
give to others—not so much in material gifts as the gifts of
compassion, sincerity, understanding. It is instilling courage
in someone else. It is the transfer of some of our self-respect
to others. It is the sharing of our confidence in ourselves
with others. It is the gift of what we are to others.

We must remember others, meeting them more than halfway, giving the best that we are. Only in this way will we
be entitled to receive friendship in return.

The English writer Samuel Johnson believed that a man
should constantly repair the quality of his friendships, and
"on clean shirt days" he went to see his friends.

We must constantly work at repairing our friendships for
others.

And we must constantly work at repairing our friendship for ourselves. As we said in the very first chapter, we
must think of ourselves as "someone we'd like to be friends
with." Because to be friendly to others we must be friendly
to ourselves. We must always be ready to repair the damage
which our failures inflict upon our self-image. We must rise
above these failures to maintain our self-respect, which is
basic to our respect for others.

Only then can our friendship have true value. Only then
can it be humble, free of aggrandizement. Only when we
respect ourselves can we feel the gift of humility—to others
and to ourselves.

If you know the art of friendship, you stay alive. You put
a smile of contentment on your self-image.

You look forward, not backward. Every day is a new day
in which you focus on life. You concentrate on your assets
for the new day, refusing to let fear of failure sidetrack you.

You have foresight. You are part of the human family;
you become what you are in relation to others. You expand

in your capacity for love in a vast communal sense which incorporates the acceptance of human fallibility. You understand that your neighbor can make errors that distort his perspective; he can mistakenly feel that you are his enemy, not his friend.

You forgive.

The whole world is looking for friendship. Everyone seeks forgiveness as ardently as he seeks food and shelter. Yet often we are ashamed to forgive as we are ashamed to make a mistake, as if it were a terrible weakness to make a mistake or forgive. But this shame corrodes us, dehumanizes us. It is unhealthy to be ashamed of error in yourself and stubborn not to forgive error in someone else.

The capacity to forgive should be as great as the capacity to survive because you cannot attain true stature in living unless you make as much a habit of forgiving as of eating.

To really get along with people requires the compassion of forgiveness. To err is human loss; to forgive is human achievement. But, first, you must forgive yourself so that you can accept yourself as a human being, as a *somebody* with dignity.

Don't Wear a Poker Face

I know four women who meet every week—in one of their homes—on Friday after dinner. For many years they have done this.

They are quite unusual. When they get together, they don't smoke, they don't drink, they don't gossip. They are so fascinated with what they are doing that they don't talk about children, husbands, relatives, the weather, politics, or world affairs.

Sitting around the table, they carry on their business as if it were the only thing in the world that mattered on their Friday evenings.

What do they do at the table? They don't knit. They are all on the plumpish side and all have their hair dyed blonde; one parted in the middle, another with a curl in the back, one with bangs, and the other with an upsweep.

They sit around the table and go about their business,

which is cards; poker, dealer's choice. None of them play it cagey; all are liberal players and sometimes reckless, too.

Over the years they have learned to know each other's game. Each has her special secret knowledge, the knowledge of the other's facial expression when she is holding a winning hand. One coughs; the second smiles; the third frowns; the last tries to look astonished.

The game goes on every Friday, year after year, and now it is at Harriet's regularly because she has arthritis and has to sit in a special chair. They play; they enjoy themselves and at the end of the year they break even.

They play poker, but they do not wear poker faces. This is their ace in the hole.

In life people too often wear poker faces and watch other people doing the same; the idea is to fool others. They corrugate the skin of their faces into all sorts of poses and affectations. But this does not work. The trick is to do what these four women do every Friday night. The trick is not to trick. Be yourself. Be true to yourself. Like yourself and let others like what you really are. Don't be affected —don't wear a poker face. Just be natural and show that you like people, that you are willing to help. Let this true face be your poker face and you will always have that ace in the hole and you will never lose.

Wives, Dogs, Money, and Enemies

Down through the centuries, if you leaf through books here and there, you can find much cutting humor on the subject of friendship.

Benjamin Franklin once wrote that "There are three faithful friends—an old wife, an old dog, and ready money."

This is not the best advertisement for friendship; it is a much better endorsement of the value of banks.

Taking leave of Louis XIV, Maréchal de Villars is supposed to have declared, "Defend me from my friends; I can defend myself from my enemies."

This is even more damning—and it is sad. Yet one cannot deny that there is a degree of truth in it.

For there are many curious relationships which go under

the name of friendship. There are alliances of convenience which people enter into without genuine commitment, and acquaintanceships which people lend themselves to without a real sense of responsibility. There are other interrelationships which are exploitative and should be labeled as such —but are not.

These are relationships from which one would do well to flee, calling for help to Louis XIV or some such protector.

But these relationships are not true friendships; they are pale facsimiles.

Friendship necessitates an inquiring mind—for others and for yourself. This does not involve sticking your nose into someone else's business or forcing your opinions on others. It means anticipating the needs of others.

It means the creative use of the imagination, not the destructive abuse of it. It is the eye of a healthy self-image, the soul of friendship. It takes inspired imagination to help others.

Rich imagination is not an exclusive gift of geniuses. It is potentially in all of us. If, daily, you long to improve yourself, to use your creative powers, you will seek enriching ideas in your mind—and you will find them. Perhaps you will share them in friendship.

Each day resolve, in your imagination, to be a good friend. What can you do for those you like? What can you say to communicate your brotherly feeling? Put yourself in the other fellow's shoes; what consideration would he appreciate?

The practice of friendship is the practice of eloquence; this eloquence needs no words since it implies an understanding of your fellow man. There is eloquence in the performance of a friendly act, done impulsively, without thought of a reward. There is eloquence in a brotherly fellow-feeling, a fellow-feeling of identification, of sharing the human condition. There is eloquence in meeting others halfway, perhaps more than halfway.

This eloquence does not belong to the few; it belongs to all of us, if we but make it one of our daily goals.

Friendship Takes Courage

Friendship requires the highest caliber of courage. This is not often recognized, but it is nonetheless true. A good friend must be a courageous person.

The usual concept of courage refers to actions under dangerous physical conditions.

We consider courageous—or brave—the man who scales perilous mountain ranges or risks his life cutting his way through snake- and crocodile-infested forests.

We consider courageous the fireman who plunges through smoke to save a child's life or the policeman who pursues a dangerous, armed criminal.

We consider courageous the combat infantryman who crawls out of his foxhole under fire to rescue a wounded buddy who is screaming for help.

These *are* acts of bravery; some are also actions for the benefit of the community. These people are heroes of our civilization, protectors of civilized life, who rise up in times of crisis.

Yet courage does not require an overt community crisis. One can be brave during the ordinary twenty-four-hour day with no flagrant dangers, but with a variety of small dangers lurking behind the minutes.

It takes real courage to attain the stature of friend to your brothers and sisters on earth. You show courage when you meet life every day with self-control. You do not attack a man for the color of his skin or the size of his nose or when he is more convincing in an argument than you are. You fight off self-aggrandizing tendencies when they would fracture the ego of someone else. You withstand the urges toward uncontrolled greed, deceit, ingratitude, conceit, malice, and disdain; you refuse to find fault with others to bolster your own sense of inadequacy.

You try to be a friend.

Friendship means you must courageously move toward your fellow men, not retreat from them as in passive living. It forbids indifference toward others. It means that you stand up and fight not only for your own beliefs but the beliefs of others. Only the brave can enter into such demanding relationships as these.

Let your energy flow away from yourself to others less fortunate, helping them willingly with your compassionate hand. Have the courage to keep moving toward life, toward people, in spite of problems, frustrations, defeats. Be strong enough to give to others in a spirit of equality. Be determined enough so that you can overcome your negative feelings; if you can't, you will not be a friend to yourself or to others. Friendship is a reaffirmation of the life instinct; it is the personification of the fighting life force.

Friendship is an exciting voyage of discovery of the good in yourself and in others. It is a daily search that never ends, a search for giving in yourself and in others—a full-time job.

A Source of Strength for You

You must be courageous to be a good friend, and to be courageous you must be strong.

You try to be strong; you try your very best. You try to see yourself in your best moments; you try to strengthen your self-image and activate the goal-minded ondriving of your success mechanism. But you are not perfect; no one is. Your thoughts become blocked, your image of yourself falters, you are no friend to yourself for the moment. What now?

Let me tell you another story. I like to tell stories and as my reader you must indulge me—just as I would like to give you every opportunity for the exploration of your own personality.

I was quite a few years younger when a friend asked me to perform an operation on his young niece who lived on the island of San Miguel in the Azores, off the coast of Portugal.

My friend was a coffee broker in Rio de Janeiro. We had formed a fervent friendship a number of years before when, meeting on a beat-up DC-3 plane bound for Rio, we had faced near-death together; the plane, overloaded and with only one good engine, had to make a forced landing in an airport hacked out of the jungle.

I could not refuse my friend's request.

A plane took us across the ocean to San Miguel—this time without mishap. At the airport were the little girl's family, a horde of handsome, friendly people—all except one. He was small, unattractive; strangely, his name was Hercules.

I had to laugh at the inappropriateness of his name. I am not tall, but I towered over—Hercules.

The little girl, Rose, was a charming child and I operated on her; a tumor on her eyelid. She was a cooperative patient; ten days after the operation, I removed the bandages and she was fine.

During those ten days I toured the island of San Miguel with Hercules.

To my surprise, Hercules was a very respected figure among the people on the island. He was well liked and admired for his wisdom. As I got to know him, I saw why: he had inordinate common sense. Everyone who had problems would come to ask his advice. I came to respect him.

One day Hercules took me by the arm and led me to the most precious sight in the Azores. The famous Furnas geysers—a valley of steam lifting out of the lovely green island. The steam poured out and up, up into the air.

Hercules commented on the luck of the people of San Miguel to have these geysers and to have such creamy rich soil and such clean air to breathe. "Man, too," he asked me, "isn't man like an island?"

I was listening with interest. What was his point?

Then I understood what he meant. The erruptions of the geysers, their letting off steam, this kept the island pure and sweet. If man, instead of bottling his feelings up inside him, would also let off steam when he needed to, he too would remain youthful and fertile and growing and successful— like the island with its geysers.

I thought of this on the plane back to New York, and I felt wiser for meeting Hercules.

Please do not misinterpret my advice. I do not recommend that you seize hold of life with a series of temper tantrums, that you blow off in all directions whenever the urge comes upon you.

My point is that friendship also means the capacity to let off steam—to let go of your pent-up emotions of resentment and hurt feelings—to find your goal of peace and quiet. Only then are you prepared for friendship with others.

In this complicated world, sometimes the wheels stop grinding and the machine comes to a halt; you can't find the oil and there's no place to go. At such times get things out, if you can do so safely, and then, cleansed, you will feel ready to reset your goals and move once more toward new adventures in success.

The "Round Table" of Givingness

Recently I lectured to the Million Dollar Round Table in Boston. This is a worldwide organization of outstanding life insurance salesmen, professionals who each year sell a million dollars or more of new life insurance policies, under strict regulations, and who conform to high ethical standards in giving service to the public which trusts them.

Before my lecture, I spoke to a number of these people and I could easily see why they were so successful. They were—friendly. They asked me about my health, my ideas, my interests—and each one *listened* to what I had to say. Too often a conversation consists of people who listen reluctantly, each waiting for his chance to talk. These people *listened* and were *interested*. Most of them made me feel I was their friend.

And so I was, for they were *friendly*.

Later, I stood on the speaker's platform and looked out over the rows and rows of faces in the auditorium—there were eighteen hundred members of the Round Table listening.

Truthfully, I felt touched; we all feel touched when others are warm.

I spoke on my concept of the "whole man." It was just another lecture, one could say, since I speak often and to groups all around the country. Yet I will always value this experience because there was so much givingness among these people. This is what I am writing about when I say that you cannot even measure the value of friendliness.

I told them how much I appreciated their being my friends.

And I did.

The Value of Friendship

Friendship is one of the great goods in life, one of its undeniable satisfactions. There can be no price on the give-and-take of friendly relating.

There can be no creative living without people—without friendship.

Anything else is a retreat from life. No sublimations, artistic or otherwise, can take the place of human relations.

No matter how busy you are, you must create time to think—about yourself, about your friendships. You must devote more effort to meeting your friends halfway, to effecting those compromises which are the heart of giving friendship, bridging the ego-gap which so often destroys.

You must create time to think of ways to make your friends happy, little considerate ways that will make them know that you are thinking of their welfare, that you care what happens to them, that you want them to live well.

But, friendship doesn't mean simply doing something for others; it involves enjoying others. Not doing someone a favor, but enjoying others without needing a reward for services rendered. The feeling of sharing is a reward in itself.

You must also create time to improve your self-friendship, to be charitable of your faults, to forgive your past blunders, to see your successes.

Yes, you must work at your most important friendship—with yourself. You must work at balancing off life's afflictions and sweetnesses, at coming to grips with a realistic, yet positive image of yourself.

To repeat, *to be a good friend, you must first be a friend to yourself.*

There is no other possibility; anything else is pretense.

Look at yourself. What do you see? Arrogance, rage, fear, tension, incompetence, poor judgment?

Of course, you are a human being, and you must not wear blinders. But do you also see these qualities in yourself? Clear thinking, confidence, compassion, humility, courage?

Be a friend to yourself, be a buddy—to yourself. Forgive your negative qualities, rise above them to your assets.

Appreciate yourself, appreciate the value of your life.

Be good to yourself; be a friend.

All the health that is in you, bring this health to your image of yourself as you live now.

As you would reach into your wallet or pocketbook and take out some money when you need it, reach into your memory and take out your inner wealth, your successful image of yourself.

It is even better than money; it is even more valuable.

Forgive and construct; forgive and construct; over and over, accentuate your best—just as you would do for a friend.

Once you are a friend to yourself, you can then be a friend to others.

You can know the joy that comes only from giving. To yourself and to those you love—your friends.

Exercise 11

Most of these exercises have been solitary; they need not all be so.

You can also help strengthen yourself for creative living if you talk over some of the concepts in this book with your friend or friends. I feel that this can be most helpful to you.

But I must caution you to use discretion: a casual acquaintance is not a friend in the tried-and-tested meaning of "friend." You should discuss these concepts only with a person who is understanding and who you feel sure is loyal to your interests.

Not that your discussion has to be personal; you may, if you wish, discuss these concepts in a general way. If your conversation bolsters your understanding of these ideas, you will be able to apply them with even greater intensity in doing the other exercises.

What can you discuss with your friends?

1. *The success mechanism.* In your interchange, you can thrash out the ingredients that make up this accelerating feeling of going forward. You can cement your conviction that these inner qualities are more important to you—both of you—than the satellites spinning around in outer space.

2. *The self-image.* As you talk, you can more clearly see why this simple concept can be so vital to your well-being. You can see why "luck" is of no consequence compared to this sense of being pleased with yourself under all circumstances.

3. *Negative feelings.* You can escalate your war against negative feelings if you can discuss with a friend the damage that such intangible emotions can do. We tend to discount the significance of thoughts and emotions—you can't see their size as you can a suspension bridge or a skyscraper—so that it could be helpful to talk about how very important they really are. When you turn your back on negative feelings, you change your "luck."

Try it with a friend.

If you know someone you can really talk to, bolstering each other as you relate, you can reinforce each other in your growing awareness of the inner factors which can lead you toward an inner-and-outer dynamic living pattern.

Not for yesterday or tomorrow.

For today.

Exercise 11A

Here is a bonus exercise for you—for when you feel frustrated.

Sit down, close your eyes, and see once again the story of Hercules. Imagine the Furnas geysers, the steam rising in the air.

Let this be a symbol for you, in your frustration, to let go of your tensions for the moment, to break the electric circuit of distress so that you can renew your energies.

Admit your anger without guilt. If you can find a harmless outlet, release these feelings of frustration. Let off steam if you can.

Then, refreshed, get back to things.

You will be a better friend—to yourself and others.

· 13 ·

Conquering the
Scourge of Loneliness

THERE ARE many things that men fear: there is war, and the weapons of war; there is disease in all its deadly forms; there is death, of oneself or of one's loved ones; there is poverty, bringing with it material deprivation and emotional humiliation; there is sudden catastrophe, striking in the night.

Men fear because they are human and therefore vulnerable. They live with their fears and do the best they can.

But of all these fears, none is more terrifying than the fear of loneliness.

Millions and millions of people would undergo almost any torture if the suffering would alleviate this most pressing fear: loneliness.

When the feeling of loneliness submerges a person, he will go to great lengths to overcome it. He will see people whom he doesn't really like, make himself subservient to people who bore him, engage in activities which he would otherwise see as a waste of time.

Moreover, he will synthetically try to overcome his feeling of loneliness by watching television, listening to the radio, playing back the tape recorder. He may finally have to resort to eavesdropping on his neighbors' quarrels.

A number of organizations try to deal with this problem, bringing people together in social settings of one kind or another. How successful they are I do not know.

What I do know is the universality of this problem. Its

conquest is far more important than that of Mount Everest or any other mountain peak; its conquest is, in my opinion, far more significant than the conquests of the North and South Poles, or any past, present, and future conquests of outer space.

First, let us define the word itself; what does *loneliness* mean?

The Meaning of Loneliness

Loneliness means different things to different people. Many people think of loneliness as being alone, in the physical sense; if one sits alone in his room, meditating, one is therefore lonely.

I disagree with this conception. The lonely person may rarely be physically by himself; he may spend most of his time with other people; he may never know what it means to spend an evening home, smoking his pipe (or knitting), thinking.

The problem of loneliness is not one of *being* alone; it is one of *feeling* alone. It is one of feeling cut off from others. It is the horrible feeling that a chasm separates one from the others, that other people are walking around in a world alien to oneself.

Many people have remarked that they feel most alone in large crowds of people where feelings of genuine closeness are lacking. Cocktails, noise, blaring music may be petty camouflage when they hide a lack of real human contact, when they obscure the human need to make a meaningful connection with other people.

On the other hand, Henry David Thoreau is the classic example of physical solitude without the tortures of loneliness. Thoreau, the great American essayist-philosopher, spent long stretches of time alone at Walden Pond, writing, thinking, enjoying his feelings of living freely, without restrictions, among the beauties of nature.

The writer and observer of social manners, Henry James, is another man who remarked that, although often alone, this did not mean he was lonely.

I knew a man like this, who spent the greater part of his

life in the frozen wastes up North, in Iceland. His companions were few—there was mostly snow and ice and barren land—but he was cheerful.

There were no prisons up there, and boys who committed offenses against society were put under his supervision; it was a long-range supervision because he put them to work on farms fifty and one hundred miles away from his cabin, but he nevertheless helped them with his kindness and by instilling in them a sense of the dignity of manual labor. Many of these boys changed in basic ways and became good members of society.

Serving humanity as he did, this man felt a sense of self-esteem, a proud connection with other people, so that he did not feel lonely.

He enjoyed simple activities such as smoking his pipe or reading a book; when he saw his boys, he advised them quietly and listened to their reports of their progress in their work and in their feelings. When he met other people, he would tell stories and enjoy their company.

But when he was alone, even for days at a time, he was never lonely. With not one other human being in sight, he was not lonely.

This is the way it should be with all people.

And yet, as medical progress enables people to live longer lives and as the world's population increases, the problem of loneliness is more acute.

This terrible *feeling* of being alone.

There can be no creative living coexisting with a feeling of loneliness; therefore, let us look at the symptoms of loneliness and see what we can do about them.

The Limitations of Loneliness

It is important for any person to accept his limitations. The person who feels he must be perfect is licked before he starts; if he is brilliant in what he attempts, his achievements may be considerable, but he is vulnerable because even the slightest failures will rob him of his peace of mind. Accomplishments that make others gasp with envy will not satisfy him; he cannot win.

Still, loneliness means *over*-limitation; it implies excessive restriction. The lonely person constricts himself unnecessarily; his life becomes too narrow. Everyone needs to channel his efforts to live in a technological civilization, but the lonely person overdoes it. There is no room for movement.

Consider a man who has purchased a plot of land—two acres. He has built a house on it for his family, and his face lights up with joy as he plans for the future; he builds a fence around his beloved two acres to serve notice to his neighbors, to his community, to his little world that this land is his.

Next he uproots the earth and plants seeds; when spring arrives, the birds chirp and the sun shines; the earth gives him back fruit, vegetables, and colorful flowers. It is Sunday and he mows the lawn, dressed simply in slacks and shirt, chatting with his neighbors and smoking his pipe.

Although he has built a fence around his land, this is not really a restriction or a constriction. He walks over to his neighbor's house to enjoy a hot meat sandwich and a cold glass of beer. His fence is not a symbol of containment, but of contentment.

The limitations of loneliness are different in that here the fence is more restricting. This fence with which we enclose ourselves keeps us from our neighbors. The claim we stake is useless; no flowers, vegetables, or fruits grow on this barren land. Love and brotherly-sisterly feeling do not flourish.

There is nothing wrong with limiting ourselves so that we do not blunder beyond our resources, but at the same time we must not limit ourselves below our capabilities. Generally, we are better than the ironclad limitations that we put on ourselves. There is a vast difference between the unwise aspiration to go beyond ourselves and the true aspiration to know ourselves. And true aspiration is the opposite of the limiting process that is part of loneliness. The reverse of limitation is extension out into the world; this should be our goal. Indeed, this is our cure.

Stubbornness and Loneliness

There is no greater weakness than stubbornness because it is the stubborn internal and external friction, internal-external resistance, and tension-building that is likely to explode in a violence that leads to failure-frustration-failure-frustration.

The stubborn man is always sure of everything and, not content to know all the answers, forces his opinions on others. He alienates others, drives them away from him. He loses a sense of give-and-take with others and feels lonely. He is usually self-righteous enough so that he does not even understand why people do not desire rapport with him, blames them, and opens up an endless chasm separating him —in his feelings—from other people.

In the *Iliad,* Homer said:

> The Gods that unrelenting breast
> have stealed,
> And cursed thee with a mind that
> cannot yield.

If you cannot "yield," if you cannot learn that there must be compromise in life—you lose. Your obstinacy robs you of pleasant relations with others.

The stubborn person curbs his own freedom, curbs the freedom of his friends, wins all arguments with everybody on every subject—and loses all his friends.

It is a sorrowful, pathetic fact that it is difficult for him to change his attitudes.

Because, even within the death-in-life of his loneliness, he knows that he is right.

The Self-Eviction of the Lonely Person

Eviction is one of the negative words in our language; it suggests poverty, a ruthless landlord, furniture on the streets, tears.

Eviction of self is even more negative; it involves an excruciating self-denial, a fundamental disbelief in ourselves, which is at the heart of loneliness. When we deliberately decide to avoid people and life, we evict ourselves from their world; as our landlord, we choose to throw our feelings, our joys back upon ourselves until they lose their meaning in the life process.

This is a defensive move, it is true, stemming from a malignant self-hatred that festers inside—a volcano of self-criticism that never explodes, never gets out into the open for healthy self-criticism.

It is a frightened, self-protective move which shows lack of faith: lack of faith in oneself, in others, in God. The self-evicting person feels keenly his own worthlessness and prefers the defensive fenced-in "quiet desperation" of loneliness to exposure—in the wholesome light—of what a monster he feels that he is.

People do not initiate this process in avoiding the self-evicting person; he avoids people, who represent to him, in large measure, eyes who see his shame, his guilt, the horror of what he is. And so, evicting his sense of self, evicting his sense of other human beings, he retreats from life into a desert of despair, into a prison of sulking and suffering, a prison far worse in reality than the prisons which house people who have committed *real* crimes against society.

The antithesis of eviction is conviction, which implies a fervent belief in ourselves. Conviction tells us that no matter how small we feel we are, we do not deserve to be cast out from the apartment of life into the gutter. Let us fill ourselves daily with the conviction that somewhere there is a place for us with others. Let us fill ourselves with it as each day we fill ourselves with nourishing food; let it become part of our daily diet.

Make a habit of this type of thinking, this type of imaging —seeing again and again our successes, forgiving our failures—and this conviction that you are a human being of dignity, of worth, that you can be proud of yourself, will make you walk back from loneliness in your heart to the world of people—where you belong.

Grief and Loneliness

Grief brings loneliness. There is an ancient Greek saying that of all ills common to all men, the greatest is grief. None of us can escape it. It makes some men tender and compassionate; others, not as strong perhaps, it makes hard, encased in protective armor.

Earlier I wrote about the tragic death of my father and of my agony. Finally, I terminated my self-imposed separation from others and returned to the world of people.

We can suffer up to a point. The body can endure so much torment; then no more. It is fitting; it is a need of the soul to grieve for a loved one lost, but the time must come when we stop grieving and return to the joyful business of living. For endless grief becomes a self-destructive force which must be stopped, like a leak in a roof; otherwise there will be a flood and enormous loss in its wake.

Endless obsession over pain means a separation from other people; it means loneliness.

Shakespeare believed that everyone can master a grief, but he that feels it; nevertheless we must master our sorrows. Time will help us if we help time; the thing to remember is that we must eventually shake off our grief and return to the everyday realities—before the inner scar becomes permanent. When this happens, we have an illness—worse than an ulcer—which we contract deep inside ourselves, bathing in a form of selfishness that is unpleasant and leads to a feeling of loneliness. Then one may find some false pleasure indulging in grief, proving Samuel Johnson's contention that grief can be a species of idleness.

The cure for grief is movement toward people, reaching out toward people with the richest qualities you have in you to give, breaking down the wall of separateness that is the fence behind which the lonely person hides.

It may be helpful to remember the words of the British statesman Benjamin Disraeli: "Grief is the agony of an instant; the indulgence of grief the blunder of a lifetime."

The Threat of Spiritual Impotence

By spiritual impotence I mean lack of emotional potency, lack of willpower and drive—and those qualities brew loneliness just as surely as tea bags in boiling water brew tea.

The spiritually impotent person can live only with the *status quo;* when change alarms him, he buries his head in the sand and runs away from life, which is too threatening for him. A feeling of loneliness results.

Emotional potency comes from an awareness that life is never static, that each day is a new one, involving changes and fresh challenges. We understand that we must accept change—even though it may breed anxiety—and that we must gear our resources to meet the challenges. In the process of facing up to these demands, we improve ourselves as human beings, developing traits such as resiliency, adaptability, versatility.

The spiritually impotent person does not understand himself and does not grasp the nature of the fluid, ever-changing quality of life. In the chasm that opens up between his non-moving ways and the swift pace of the world moving around him lies the cause of his feeling of separateness from others, of dissociation from life.

There is hope for him, as there is for every individual. It resides in his strengthening of his opinion of himself, in seeing his better qualities, in emphasizing and visualizing these qualities until they become part of his image of himself.

When he is no longer afraid of what he has always considered his lack, when he no longer feels a need to apologize for his existence, when he can tolerate change in himself, then he will feel equipped to cope with changes in the big world outside.

The Illusion in Nostalgia

When life is oppressive, when the alarm clock summons you to insoluble problems and unending worries, it is natural to long for escape from a reality that seems unbearable.

We begin to daydream, to think of some sunny island paradise—maybe we've seen it in an advertisement or on a postcard or in a movie—and to wish we were there. Or perhaps our minds bring back an image of a pleasant place we knew when we were very young and when life seemed to be less complicated.

Such temporary escapes (into a room in your mind, into an Ischia in your mind) may be helpful in giving us relief from tension.

But the habit of continually escaping from reality—into the past—is unfruitful and unproductive. It ends up as a flight from mature thinking into a barren pattern which may be mostly illusion, anyway.

The nostalgic person comes to separate himself from the living which must be most important to him, the living of today for the sake of today, with each day something special —even if it is imperfect. The more intense his nostalgia for the "good old days," the more false his picture of these days is likely to be; if the pattern becomes fixed, his thinking may end up 90 percent illusion. He feels lonely because his thinking has isolated him from his fellows.

The cure for the Old Nostalgia is the New Nostalgia. The New Nostalgia is a creative kind of longing; the longing is not for yesterday, but for today and tomorrow. It is a longing to improve ourselves—for today and tomorrow—and to make a habit of it. As part of this self-improvement, we must know ourselves better and befriend ourselves more consistently. The New Nostalgia is a longing to know what we are made of *now,* not what we were made of many yesterdays ago. It is an intense desire to avoid the pitfalls of our failure mechanism, to reactivate the smooth functioning of our success mechanism, so that we can live richer lives each day. It is a determination to make our days creative, full of good feeling with other people, of fun.

Nostalgia for the past, in addition to being frequently illusory, can be a deadly trap. It may bring on moping, years of loneliness, and pathetic self-indulgence. Do not let this happen to you!

The New Nostalgia, that's a different story.

Separation and Loneliness

We have dissected the symptoms of loneliness, as I see it, and have found: limitation, stubbornness, self-eviction, grief, spiritual impotence, nostalgia. These are basic components of loneliness, as basic as are sugar, flour, and eggs if you want to bake a cake.

Last let us discuss separation, or the feeling of being separate.

Not separation in terms of time or space, but in terms of *feeling*.

I do not know if I would call the feeling of separation a symptom of loneliness; perhaps it would be more accurate to say that the feeling that one is separate, cut off from other people, unable to reach out and touch others because there is an unbridgeable gap between them—is loneliness itself.

For loneliness, the feeling of loneliness, is this terrible feeling of separateness from one's fellow brothers, of isolation from one's clan.

This is a terrible feeling, just about the most agonizing feeling that there is.

I believe, and I do not think this thought has originated with me, that people who are terrified of death think of it as a complete separation from others—rather than as a continuation or a rejoining or part of a natural process.

It is not the thought of death that frightens them; it is the fear of separation, of an eternal loneliness.

People who do not fear death have lived rich lives. They have lived close to other people all their lives, and to them death must seem a continuation of this happy state—with firm imprints they have left behind in the workaday world as fond consecrations to their lives.

Separation, loneliness, these are the scourges. These are man's great terrors.

The man who goes into battle—an infantryman stalking the enemy with rifle and grenade—goes forward with his buddies, feeling a close sense of comradeship which enables him to overcome his terror of death and keep moving forward. He is frightened, but is he *as* frightened as the lonely person who has no friends, no one to talk to, emptiness in his soul and who, with no realistic dangers, is afraid to go out and meet people in the light of day?

Grim as his lot is, the infantryman at least knows that he is doing his best, that he is meeting reality, that his friends will help him if they can.

Exercise 12

All right, you are trying to plan pleasure into your days. One of the most formidable obstacles to pleasure is the problem of loneliness.

Certainly literature on the subject would testify, almost pathetically, to the fact that in today's world the feeling of loneliness is a grave problem.

What can you do about it?

A great deal.

You can work hard at a job that needs to be done: elimination of symptoms of loneliness.

1. You can work to stop imposing unreasonable limitations on yourself.

2. You can try to be less stubborn, to see the other fellow's point of view once in awhile.

3. You can take up legitimate tenancy in your own mind and work at securing your position there, refusing to evict your feelings of belonging and of self-respect.

4. You can combat feelings of grief that threaten to submerge all your more joyful life instincts.

5. You can take up arms against a feeling of spiritual impotence if you will fortify your sense of being able to deal with a changing, uncertain world.

6. You can drown the outdated nostalgia for the past in a New Nostalgia, in a longing for good days now and tomorrow. You can work to realize these worthwhile longings.

Every day, when you can spare a few minutes, run down this list of the components of loneliness. Which apply to you? Use a mental mirror so that you can see yourself as objectively as is possible. Be honest—even if it hurts. What are the factors which separate you from other people—and from your sense of self? Look in your real mirror when it is natural; look in your mental mirror also to help yourself.

Every day make strong efforts to find the reasons you feel lonely and to strengthen your feelings of being a good human being, an interconnected member of the human race.

See if this effort won't help you.

But, more than anything, you can work to put into sharper focus your happy image of yourself. You can work to go forward into each day with more confidence—with a stronger self-image.

I cannot repeat this concept enough, this concept of your self-image, because this is your best friend or your worst enemy.

If you strengthen your self-image, if you do it realistically, with no magic, no sham, no phoniness, by building on a friendly estimate of what you are now, projecting this into what you can be as you strengthen your thinking and imaging, you will make great strides in many basic areas of your life.

Accepting yourself, you will accept others and take steps to overcome the chasm between you which constitutes loneliness.

You can conquer loneliness.

Once you have done this, you can live creatively.

You will feel a sense of closeness, of brotherliness, toward your fellow human beings—and surely this is one of the keys to the happy life.

Also practice over again *Exercise* 11 in the previous chapter. *Do* it, *do* it, over and over again..

• 14 •

Creative Living at
Sixty-Five and Over

TWO FRIENDS meet in front of a supermarket in a comfortable surburban area; they shake hands. They're both over sixty and their conversation goes like this.

"How are you, Joe? Good to see you."

"As well as could be expected, Jim, at my age. How are you?"

"Same as you, Joe, you know how it is. Any day I don't have aches and pains, that's a good day. When I was younger, I expected more—but now I know better. No aches in my legs today. I'm keeping my fingers crossed."

"I have to do the shopping for the wife these days, her back is worse. See you, Jim."

"All right, Joe."

This conversation is no original production of mine—I've heard it before and so have you. It reflects the type of thinking which plunges people in their sixties and over into a prison of their own making, a jail in which pain and disease is the warden, in which the bars are fears about chronological age—numbers—and of death.

Since creative living is rare among people over sixty-five suppose we devote just one chapter to the special problems of these retirement-age people. I feel that this chapter should also be interesting for younger people; it may help them to feel more optimistic about the possibilities for happiness in their later years.

Because at any age, you can still lead a good life. Contrary to popular belief, happiness is not a chronological numbering process.

The Dread Number "65"

Yet, incredibly, these numbers do carry grave emotional overtones. The book *Life Begins at Forty* may have helped lift the ceiling on worrying about age, like a moratorium on debts, but the number sixty-five remains a deadly number. This is partly a socioeconomic factor: many business corporations, seeing sixty-five symbolizing the end of man's value as an economic producer, have established this age as one of compulsory retirement. At any rate sixty-five is not a number to ring out in musical chimes; it may soon threaten the status of "13" as the unmentionable numeral.

Many people, at sixty-five, tell themselves that life is over. They think constantly about death and talk about physical symptoms that could cause death. Each day becomes a delaying action against the forces of death instead of a dedication to enjoying life. Their thoughts brim over with fear, and their conversation is a recital of the deaths and illnesses of friends and relatives.

Worry swoops around in their minds like pigeons descending upon thrown breadcrumbs, and they spend the rest of their years of life living with death.

Others reach sixty-five and collapse in a kind of rosy inertia. They have, they feel, reached the sunshine years and are entitled to years and years of retirement. They will sleep at night and take catnaps during the day; they will lie in their beds at night and occupy deck chairs in the daytime. Their attitude toward everything is horizontal, never vertical. They will not walk, they will ride in cars; they will not do, they will rest. They will not even think; TV or the newspapers will do their thinking for them. Surely after their years of struggle, making money to pay the bills, raising children, these retirement years will be glorious.

The number sixty-five is deadly to these people. They —is it you?—waste their time fearing death, since death is a natural process which they can do nothing about. They— is it you?—will not enjoy a retirement from life, for this is a premature death.

Some younger pepole—is it you?—dissipate their productive energies in worry about what will happen to them when they come face to face with the monstrosity of age sixty-five.

While you have the privilege of life on this earth—and it is a privilege, in spite of the unceasing problems—you should live. You should live, whether you are sixteen or sixty-five.

Be like Ezio Pinza, an inspiration to millions when he starred in "South Pacific," reaching the peak of his career at an age when many people retire. Pinza was young when others his age force themselves to decay; he was far younger in spirit than some less fortunate people in their early twenties.

Naturally, older age requires that a person place sensible limits on his physical capabilities. When you are older, you can't run around like a young kid and, if you have a heart condition, you must further restrict your activities. Yet, the older person often has qualities that the child or the adolescent hasn't even begun to develop.

The main point is: *In older age each day can still be thrilling.*

It's really up to the individual. It's up to you.

Still, if you are over sixty-five and have already wasted time moping, don't blame yourself for it. You're not perfect, no one is, and self-blame will not help you. Just read what I have to say and see if my ideas won't help you to live more meaningfully.

The Spiritual Suicide of Old Age

One of the chief threats to an older person's self-image is the negative attitude of many people toward his usefulness as a member of the community. If an older person allows others' attitudes to influence his own thinking (and to be swallowed up is easy), he will sit out years, moping and complaining, passive and vegetative. He will commit a form of spiritual suicide which is one of the tragedies of our times.

I have known a number of people who lived contentedly until they were about sixty-five, satisfied with themselves, with what they got out of life, with what they gave to life.

Then, abruptly, they cut themselves loose from their strengths. Their golden years were over, they felt, so what could they do? Other people did not regard them in the same way; they were no longer useful. Now they were excess baggage. Why pretend?

There was some reality to their observations because in our culture, and many other cultures, older people are denied credit for their genuine resources and abilities.

These unfortunate attitudes are real and you must know what is real, but, when you are older, do you have to accept them?

Do you have to follow the herd and uncritically accept the ideas of the herd when these ideas are foolish?

Of course you don't!

Respect for Age

When a person grows up in a culture, he generally adopts the customs of that culture uncritically. If an American, he will probably play baseball; if an Englishman, it will be cricket; if he comes from Switzerland, he will more probably be adept at skiing.

Ways of thinking—attitudes toward old age, for example —which we take for granted, are not necessarily universal concepts.

In Confucian-oriented cultures there is reverance for age. Confucius, the great Chinese social thinker, whose goal was a good society based on kindness and loyalty, made an impact on Chinese ethics, government, and religion which lasted for two thousand years in China and spread to other countries as well.

"The truly virtuous man," Confucious wrote, "desiring to be established himself, seeks to establish others; desiring success for himself, he strives to help others succeed ... Virtue is to love men."

Confucius was in favor of a society bound together with moral obligations: father-and-son, husband-and-wife, friend-and-friend. He stressed continuity of people, which led to strong family bonds involving filial piety, respect for age, and ancestral worship. The ancestral rites were to be performed sincerely, to continue the human relationship which death should not terminate, and to remind people of the beginning of their lives, which would enable them to feel connected and virtuous.

Some scholars feel that, though Confucius was a learned man, his book wisdom has been exaggerated—but I do not believe anyone questions the intensity of his compassion for people.

His ideas took root in cultures which, with all their imperfections, stressed a respectful appreciation of the positive qualities of older people.

Although his influence is waning, his ideas are still important in a few countries, such as Japan, in which the family is a continuing entity, and veneration for older people survives.

Older people are valued in other cultures for economic reasons, mostly.

This situation prevails among some groups of Eskimos, where men may hunt till they are seventy and women are needed all their lives for the skill of their domestic accomplishments: picking vegetables, preserving meat, sewing winter clothing, and passing on to their grandchildren, whom they entertain at length, the tall stories of their ancestors.

Even after seventy, men are highly respected among these Eskimos for their know-how in judging weather, ice, and current movements, as well as the habits of polar animals. Younger men look to their elders for guidance in dealing with environmental factors which they are too young to have mastered. There have been stories of village elders saving other men's lives through their ability to navigate boats through impenetrable fog past ice floes to safety.

These Eskimo elder citizens are valued for their productive economic role; in sections of Burma, older people receive homage for the contributions they made to society when they were younger. As older people, they are free to indulge in meditations and philosophy, while they maintain their influence as wise counselors of their families and receive the respectful support of their children, who honor them for their lifetime of service as loving parents.

My point in describing these foreign cultures is certainly not that they are better than ours—they are infinitely more primitive and in some ways are much more cruel—but that they are different in their concept of the value of older people. The study of other people's ideas can lead us to change ours, sometimes, just in showing us that ours are not the only possible ideas.

"When in Rome, do as the Romans do," it is said, but then there are different kinds of Romans.

The Dignity of Your Later Years

Generalizations are rarely black-and-white accurate. You will surely find people who respect old age and who have positive attitudes toward its fulfillment, toward its wisdom and dignity. When I criticize modern attitudes, I criticize the norm. There are always exceptions.

To be fair to our present-day culture, negative attitudes toward older people prevailed in many past cultures, too.

I do not often watch television, but several years ago I saw a TV play whose images—historically accurate, I assume—have remained sharply focused in my mind. The action took place perhaps fifty or sixty years ago in the Old West.

An Indian tribe took an old Indian—no longer useful, they thought—to a cave to die, since the medicine man thought he was an evil influence. The cowboys tried to save the old Indian but failed. Then the rivers dried up and everyone despaired for the future. As a last resort the old man was able to call on his store of wisdom. He was the only one consulted who remembered how this had happened many years before, and how the tribe was able to release the river waters at that time by digging around a certain clump of rocks. With the old man's help, the river waters flowed once more and his grateful Indian brothers took him back to their settlement to live.

But when his friends the cowboys moved on, the medicine man had his way again. The old man was sent back to the cave to await death. Medicine-man superstitions had outweighed his proven value to his community.

The wise old Indian—so valued when he was young—just stared at the walls of his cave-prison, and the scene was sad enough to bring tears to my eyes.

What a waste! What intolerable ignorance and inhumanity! Can one accept such practices? I cannot. It's something like the ridiculous Chinese attitude of old, devaluing the birth of girl babies, since girls were considered inferior creatures.

Or the barbarous New England crusade to burn "witches" to death.

This poor Indian—and he remains in my mind, sprawled dejectedly in his cave—is symbolic of an "in the ashcan" attitude that still holds sway over years in a person's life that should be dignified.

I am told that good wine and champagne improve with age, and it is often this way with people.

In some mathematical and engineering jobs people of sixty-five and over—even handicapped people—do at least as well as younger people.

In certain precious human qualities, older people obviously demonstrate a superiority over youth. Years of experience in life often produce greater tolerance for individual differences and for human error. Where youth is often cruel and arrogant, older people who age gracefully are infinitely more accepting—both of their fellow man and of the conditions of life in this world. Time, which poets through the years have denounced as a robber of youth, brings with it seasoned wisdom, knowledgeable contentment, rich *savoir faire.*

Civil Rights for Older People

We must get away from segregating older people into a ridiculous compartment marked OVER SIXTY-FIVE—REST, SLEEP, SUNBATHE, consigning them into a useless age bracket which demands their dignity as human beings, which destroys their hope for good living.

Is this not discrimination?

Civil rights is a big thing in this country today—and for good reason. Too long have Negroes been segregated into slums, crowded into poor schools, discriminated against economically and socially because of the color of their skins.

This racial prejudice, this segregation of all these people into one supposedly inferior compartment marked NEGRO has long been a national disgrace, and it is about time that people of influence have responded to the need for change. Actually only the first steps have been taken; more needs to be done to give to the Negro in this country his full status as a human being, his true dignity as a creature of God every bit as worthy as another person whose skin happens to be white.

I'm sure that almost all of my readers will agree with these sentiments.

Still, how about the enfeebling, soul-destroying segregation of older people? Why is there not a clamor against this, too?

Because there should be. There is youth in the old, and oldness in the young; people are complicated, and the type of categorization implicit in the over-sixty-five mumbo jumbo is absurd. Why not segregate people into short and tall, or thin and fat, encouraging the short and thin people to lead productive lives, while the tall and fat people take catnaps, watch television, and sunbathe? It would make about the same amount of sense.

Segregation of older people is unfair; it is also untruthful.

The Truth about Your Later Years

The truth about your later years is that their quality is not a chronological affair. People are people, and you can't number them and then write them off.

The truth is that they can be creative. This should be reassuring not only to older people, but to young readers who dread a future which has been misspelled for them.

Carl Sandburg, the great American poet and biographer of Abraham Lincoln, creator of such epics as *The People, Yes,* wrote some of his most noted works after the age of seventy.

The late Herbert Hoover, former U.S. President, took on the assignment of coordinating world food supplies of thirty-eight countries for President Truman in 1946—at the age of seventy-two. In 1958 he was United States representative to Belgium—at the age of eighty-four.

Charlie Chaplin, at seventy-six, was at work directing a movie with "youngsters" like Sophia Loren and Marlon Brando.

Samuel Eliot Morison capped a lifetime of distinguished historical writing with his *Oxford History of the American People,* a smash best-seller in 1965 when he was in his late seventies.

In another area, the "young man's game" of baseball, Casey Stengel at seventy-five—hair white, back slumped— finally retired from the exhausting daily assignment of managing the New York Mets.

The late great Eleanor Roosevelt was busier during her "retirement years" than many people are in their twenties and thirties, participating in community, political , and charitable activities. She even found time in her middle seventies to write her autobiography.

Another productive man who refused to slow down prematurely is Edward Steichen, the photographer-artist-plant breeder. In 1955, in his middle seventies, Steichen created the famed Family of Man exhibition for the Museum of Modern Art, certainly one of his great achievements.

In the fields of politics and government, men like the late Bernard Baruch and the late Herbert Lehman served in official and unofficial capacities until they were well into their seventies. The late Alben Barkley was Vice-President of the United States in his mid-seventies, and Dwight Eisenhower was well past the sixty-five-year-old dividing line when he relinquished the Presidency.

Pablo Casals, cellist-composer-conductor, was featured in a TV documentary showing how at eighty-eight he was still active, conducting, teaching, and working for peace.

Artists like Picasso, in his eighties, and Chagall, in his seventies, are still creating. They are not likely to retire— not voluntarily.

These people did not confiscate their talents and recoil in fright when they passed sixty-five. They paid heed to their creative life instincts, as I am sure they did when they were younger, and forgot about the numbers which their passing birthdays registered.

Still, when I think of people who lived fully in their later years, undaunted and unafraid, two men come to mind—the late Winston Churchill and the late Albert Schweitzer.

Churchill was an energetic political leader as a comparatively young man, but his greatest trials and triumphs came in his later years. Taking over as Prime Minister in May 1940, at the age of sixty-five, with Great Britain on the defensive before Nazi tyranny, he declared, "I have nothing to offer but blood, toil, tears, and sweat."

In July 1940 he rallied his people. "We will defend every village, every town, every city."

On his sixty-sixth birthday the official statement was "The Prime Minister is getting on with the war."

He "got on with the war," and no one knew he had surmounted a heart attack during these years.

Churchill at seventy addressed crowds on V-E Day plus 1, climbing on top of his car to speak.

At eighty, having been in and out of power since the war, Churchill retired as Prime Minister.

In his eighties he substituted hobbies such as painting and scholarly pursuits for politics. He lived with goals and interests, and never retired from the people of his country who so idolized him. When he died, at ninety, no one could feel sorry for him because he had used his life so well. His death was the world's loss.

Schweitzer was another marvel. Surely one of the most versatile men there ever was, Schweitzer was missionary, humanitarian, surgeon, founder of a hospital, college principal, Oxford lecturer, organist, theologian, author.

In his late seventies he was awarded the Nobel Peace Prize.

On his eightieth birthday he was as usual at Lambaréné, Gabon, French Equatorial Africa, where he founded his famous hospital for the native inhabitants. He was still active in his work, tending the sick, working on his manuscripts, playing Bach on his piano, spending the day with his friends from Africa and Europe.

Until his death at ninety, Schweitzer continued to live each day fully—and usefully.

Are these chronicles interesting to you? Are they instructive? They should be because they are refutations of the straightjacket-at-sixty-five and prison-cell-at-seventy philosophy with which people murder themselves while they are alive.

"But these men," you may say, "are extraordinary men (and women). How am I like them?"

You are in the same chronological age group as they are —or in five or ten or forty or fifty years, you will be.

"Of course," you say, "but they are famous. I am nobody. No one knows who I am."

I cannot deny this. But one's joy comes, not from fame, but from the joy of exercising one's creative powers. These people are flesh-and-blood; they are not gods. Regardless of their accomplishments, they are as human as you and I. Just as these people, in their more publicized spheres, have lived active, positive years in later life, so can you, who are free of the restrictions of fame—as well as deprived of privileges.

Recently I gave a seminar in psycho-cybernetics in San Diego, California, and one of the students was a man of eighty-two. During a recess, he came over to talk to me.

"I love your books *Psycho-Cybernetics* and *The Magic Power of Self-Image Psychology*," he said, "and I've been loaning my copies to my friends. Doctor, do you know why I'm taking this course?"

"Why?"

"Because I'm eighty-two, and I'm practicing to be ninety."

This man did now know the meaning of "retire," of "the age of anxiety," or any of our twentieth-century words of negation. An ordinary man, he knew life and renewal, he knew maturity in old age. He was a Galileo before whom new worlds opened and, like Galileo, he was not afraid to open his eyes and explore new areas of endeavor.

So can you, most of you, if you remember that the time to retire in one field is when you are growing up in another.

Exercise 13

Now, what can you do about this older-age bugaboo which is haunting us today? Sit down, relax, and let's think about it.

1. *Talk sense to yourself about age.* If you're young, fearing age sixty-five, or over sixty-five, feeling sorry for yourself, it all amounts to the same thing: all you've got to do is open your eyes, and you'll see that people are people. You'll see young people of seventy and old people of eighteen. Just forget superstitious phobias and talk sense to yourself. If you can't manage this, read again the achievements of older people which I have described for you.

2. *Fight pessimistic talk about older age.* When people tell you what a horrible thing it is to be older, refuse to let

them depress you; too long have older people denied themselves the right to live creatively. Death is closer? The satisfaction of many years of continuity weighs heavily, too. Aches and pains? Yes, but pressures are lighter, one has more time to do what one wants. Don't let anyone shove negative ideas down your throat!

3. *Set goals for yourself.* Every day you must set goals —no matter what your age. Stop losing your war with negative feelings; forget sixty-five if that's your age, or if you'll be sixty-five in thirty years, and concentrate on enjoying each day. Throw negative thoughts about age out of your mind with as much efficiency as you would dump your garbage down the incinerator. Plan your day, set your goals; tomorrow you will set more goals. Each day you will find something to enjoy.

4. *Never retire.* Say to yourself that you will never retire from the world of things you love—no matter what other people think. Tell yourself that when you must retire in one field, you will grow up in another—even a hobby is fine. But never retire from life!

5. *Give yourself the right to be happy.* You must give yourself this right at any age. Stop shortchanging yourself; stop blocking your pleasure. The "pursuit of pleasure" is your human right.

The Third Act

I must admit that this is an angry chapter. I cannot accept the blocks that people put in the way of creative living, but I feel really outraged at some of the idiotic myths which infest people's minds, destroying their hopes for their later years.

Yet it is a hopeful chapter because so much can be done to rectify these ignorant prejudices.

The Roman philosopher Cicero reflected a great deal about the later years of life, and he wrote many wise opinions on this subject. "Old Age," he believed, "is the consummation of life, just as of a play."

A good play must have a good beginning, and the second act must carry it along. But the third act must carry it to a powerful conclusion—if the play is worthwhile. A superior play must have a real punch at the end; it must send you home happy or dazzled or moved.

It is this way with life. You taste your fullest riches in your later years. Not worries, not fears, not problems—riches.

Your later years—even with your physical limitations, even with your battles against disease—can be your richest.

But, first, you must know that they can be rich.

And, second, most important, you must feel that you are worth it. You must be able to allow yourself joy.

Then, your later years, too, can be creative.

• 15 •

Your Creative Day

THIS BOOK IS about creative living. Not tomorrow, when you hope that all human problems will be solved in some utopian setting. Today. In today's world with its headaches and its heartaches, its troubles and its calamities, its joys and its satisfactions.

In today's world, with more and more people crowded into less and less space, with racial hostilities and nuclear weapons. Creative living—today.

In today's world, with its upthrusting skyscrapers, its machines shooting into outer space, its huge glass-fronted buildings. Creative living—today.

In today's world, with sex gone wild, speedy surfboarding, sensual dancing, shorter skirts for women. Creative living—today.

In our world of today, with its search for new ideas and values, its existentialism, its Zen, its rush back toward religion, its self-questioning. Creative living—today.

Now, now, in a world moving to the suburbs, with way-out shopping centers, bustling supermarkets, glamorized fashions. Creative living—today.

In today's world, with its car-crowded superhighways, its

traffic jams, water shortages, crippling strikes. Creative living—today.

In today's world, with its free exchange of ideas, its righting of ancient wrongs, its rebellion against injustices, its championing of long-oppressed peoples. Creative living—today.

In today's world, with its increased psychological knowledge, its greater awareness of human motivation, its packaging of polished entertainment. Creative living—today.

This is a most imperfect world, true, but it has its virtues, and these you must find. It has its good values, and these you must find. It has your self, and this you *must* find.

It is in today's world that you must live; it is in today's world that you must learn to lead a good life. Forget about tomorrow; think about today.

Let us make today a creative day; let us look to the day with objectives; let us regard the day as our opportunity. We must do everything we can to make each day a life in itself.

Each day we must fight off our negative feelings and the negative forces in our world, and make this day a happy one.

Creative living today means a creative *day* today. Then another good day. And another good day. One day at a time. You add up a succession of creative days—and you have a creative life.

You will not achieve this creative day with our modern-day mechanical marvels; they may help or hurt. You will achieve it if you can develop your emotional, spiritual, thinking qualities. You will achieve it if you understand what invisible qualities you need to face up to life successfully.

In the pages of this chapter, we will discuss, and spell out for you, the components of your creative day.

The Faces of Your Creative Day

St. Augustine once wrote, "The world is a book and those who don't travel read only one page." I hope you will "travel" in reading this book, but if you choose to

read just one page, here, in capsule form, are the facets of
your creative day.

1. C: *C*oncentration with courage
2. R: *R*eturn to yourself.
3. E: *E*ars for others.
4. A: *A*ffirmation.
5. T: *T*raining in self-discipline.
6. I: *I*magination.
7. V: *V* for Victory.
8. E: *E*agerness.

9. D: *D*aily growth.
10. A: *A*djustment.
11. Y: *Y*earning for improvement.

1. *Concentration with courage.* Your first step in planning
a creative day is to concentrate on it. Concentration itself
—we might call it the art of concentration—offers a problem.

That problem is how to clear your mind of all distracting
factors. Can this be done? Yes. And with a simple approach.

First let's divide up this matter of concentration.

There is long-term concentration in dieting to lose weight,
concentrating over weeks and perhaps months on this single
goal, without swerving from it.

Then there is short-term concentration, the focusing of
the mind on an immediate problem—such as living a creative day.

Think of concentration in terms of a book or a play,
with a beginning and an end. Thought must have a beginning
and an end, too. Therefore you know that there will be an
end to your thought—an answer; and you may feel sure that
by reaching that end you will be developing the mental
muscles of concentration.

A letter, too, must have a beginning and an ending. The
difficult part in writing a letter is the act of sitting down
and starting it. But, once begun, the end is in sight. Once
you have started to concentrate on what you want to do,
the end—the living of a creative day—is in sight. And,

anything that is in sight—why, you are almost there already!

Concentration is vital to your well-being. By clearing your mind of all irrelevancies, sweeping out everything except the planning of a creative day, you take dead aim at your objectives.

Concentration, then, is as simple as this: *the mere act of willing to begin.*

Begin, try, and you have solved the problem of concentration.

Thus concentration implies courage; you must be able to take off and plunge. You must feel a sense of collaboration with your internal resources, your success mechanism.

It implies emancipation—from negative feelings. You must free your self-image to grow.

Too often we enslave our thinking, bind ourselves with self-critical abuse, put chains on our thoughts, block off our feelings with walls of inhibition.

We impress ourselves with rationalizations. We dig up synthetic reasons for our needless limitations; we may even deny the possibility of productive living. We sentence ourselves to life imprisonment—our only crime is our series of blunders.

You must emancipate yourself from such thinking, which produces a shrinking of your self-image, and come to an understanding of your strength.

Many historians feel that the late President John Kennedy will grow with the years, as scholars measure his importance to the world and place him in proper perspective. If so, surely it will be a reflection of his ability to concentrate his thinking and to emancipate it from limitations. Kennedy encouraged imagination in political life and in international relations.

Your world may be much smaller in scope than was President Kennedy's—before his tragic death—but it can be just as meaningful to you as his world was to him. To live a creative day, you must first of all concentrate, with courage.

2. *Return to yourself.* In order not to retreat from life, but return to it during our creative day, we must utilize our potentialities. Thinking is our greatest gift; it is what makes us superior to the animal. Whatever our capacities, we can think within those capacities. Whatever we think our limi-

tations are, we must think clearly within those limitations we give to ourselves, and we are sure to learn that we are more than we think we are. We must learn that such understanding is not mere meditation; it is thought in action. Thinking here is not passive, but an active process.

To feel secure, we must use our brains to understand ourselves and others. As we become craftsmen in our work, to make enough money to live, we must become craftsmen in understanding. Holding our job is not enough: part of our job in life is to understand ourselves and others, to feel compassion for our faults and those of others; part of our job is to avoid the negative feelings of the past and to concentrate on our pleasures and on our successes.

Every day we must return to ourselves. Every day, after we try to cope with our problems in living, we must realize our identity as persons of worth.

We must return to ourselves with as much determination as General Douglas MacArthur when he returned in triumph to the Philippines.

Does this sound too melodramatic?

It really is not at all.

Because, in the process of living, many of us move away from ourselves, forget who we are and what we are made of. We destroy our life force as completely as an army of moths would eat up our woolens.

If we have failed in past undertakings—and all of us have—we may be fearful of failing in our present endeavors, and so we distort our perspective, our self-image, and we walk away from ourselves, walk away from what we really are and what we can be.

We desert our image of ourselves in self-hatred; we desert ourselves for a vacuum or regress to a vegetative sort of nonindividualistic, self-image-less living.

We must take time off every day—even if only ten or fifteen minutes—to take stock of ourselves, to return to ourselves, to return to our realistic self-image. We must admit our failures, but realize that they are part of the process of living. None of us is perfect; we dare not deny ourselves the opportunity to improve.

As part of your creative day, you must return into an "Ischia of your mind" for awhile and remember:

A. That you can succeed in your future undertakings as you once did in the past.

B. That you can correct mistakes and rise above failures.

C. That every day is a new lifetime and that you have to start anew to reach your goal every day.

D. That in such realization you become your own creator and plan the day for yourself constructively.

E. That negative feelings take you away from yourself and make you less than what you are.

F. That every day you must battle negative feelings and struggle to reach self-fulfillment.

G. That arrogance keeps you from yourself, from others, and from God.

H. That in returning to yourself you have the opportunity to profit by your errors; as your own plastic surgeon, without knives, you can compassionately cut away self-hatred and improve your self-image.

I. That with a strong self-image you need never retreat from life or from self.

Why is *return to self* a face of creative living?

Because if you feel this sense of inner fortification, you will not use excuses to retreat from life.

In the words of Robert Louis Stevenson, "To be what we are, and to be what we are capable of being, is the only end of life."

3. *Ears for Others.*

We must be enterprising in going toward people; we must develop the capacity to hear others. It is important for us to hear others talk, not just to hear ourselves talk.

The art of listening is the art of understanding; it is the art of progress. In this art of listening, we must think of our ears as two extra eyelids. Our eyelids open and close; they open to light and they close to irritation or possible injury. We learn to open our ears to the opinion of others; learn that others are just as good as we are even if they have faults. We have faults, too. We learn to open our ears to reason because reason very often has a difficult time in this world, and people refuse to listen to it.

There can be no enterprise without communication between people; we must at all times try to develop it.

We must have ears for ourselves, to listen to the heartbeat of our mind, to the clock within us that ticks away the joys and sorrows we are heir to, to that self-image of ours that could be our friend.

If we have to shut our ears, we learn to shut them to prejudices and prevarication, to the daily threats of negative feelings.

Enterprise is a matter of communication, of self-image strength, of going toward life without fear. In your creative day. And every day.

4. *Affirmation.* You don't resign from life, renounce it; you reaffirm it. You don't resign from your self-image, renounce it; you reaffirm it, realizing that there is no life without it.

This is a cardinal principle of everyday creative living. You reach your true potential through aspiration. You must aspire every day not only for yourself but for others—for your friends, your community, your church or temple. You must not let competitiveness blind you to your role as a member of the great human family. You must affirm your human brotherliness; the misfortunes of others must be your misfortunes. You must feel for other people.

You must assert your belief in today and in tomorrow. Life changes every day; you must vibrate each day to the inspiration of worthwhile goals, avoiding negative feelings and reactivating the success mechanism within you. I repeat this because it is basic to living.

You must free yourself from harsh moral judgments; you must equip yourself to understand and love your human brothers and sisters—if you first understand and love yourself.

A few months ago, walking down one of New York's many crowded streets, I saw a taxi wheel around a corner, then slow down, and stop to discharge a passenger. Another taxi, following around the corner, could not stop in time. There was a very mild collision.

The driver of the first cab, of course, came around to inspect the damage to the rear of his vehicle. There was none. He said "Forget it" to the other cabbie, climbed in his cab, and pulled off into the traffic—on his way to a new fare.

He could have made a big fuss—other drivers have hired lawyers for less—but his brotherly feeling for his fellow hackie was too strong. He could have caused trouble; he would not do it.

As I kept walking, going to my office, I found myself smiling at the unpretentious brotherliness of the cabdriver's conduct.

To me this represented an affirmation of the positive life force, an affirmation of reaching out to people—in the midst of the cold jungle that New York traffic can be.

It is an affirmation of good relations among people which, to a large extent, *is* life.

To live a creative day, you must assert your belief in yourself, your belief in people, your belief in the creatures of life.

5. *Training in self-discipline.* Self-discipline is your golden key: without it, you cannot be happy. Discipline is the difference between what we can do and what we should do. In our creative day we live with discipline, continuing to set goals, refusing to permit the termites of nothingness to empty us as human beings.

In my lifetime I have known many famous people—executives, statesmen, stars of stage and screen, doctors—and I have been aware of their emotional scars. Few have followed straight lines to their successes; most have blundered at times and have overcome their blunders with their persistent belief in themselves. Discipline, in the final analysis, has been the tool with which they have forged their successes; self-discipline has been their mighty weapon.

All artists are slaves to their craft before they can become masters of it. All musicians are daily slaves to practice which means self-denial; they must practice again and again if they are to succeed.

Ted Williams wanted to be a great hitter, and that's what he became, one of the greatest in baseball's history. But he did it with practice, not magic.

In the same way we must discipline ourselves if we are

to be happy. It takes discipline to set goals and to implement them.

Epictetus said: "Lead the good life and habit will make it pleasant." If we master the habit of self-discipline, the world shall be ours. And if we want to get into daily training to get the habit, here is what to do.

Close your eyes and watch me on the screen of your mind. I'm shadowboxing even though I'm not a boxer. As I punch my imaginary foe, I have learned to dance away with agility. My feet are quick, my fists are quick, my mind is quick; I have disciplined myself to defeat my enemy.

You can train yourself in the symbolic art of shadowboxing, too, for the battles you have to fight every day to make something of life, to reach your goals.

You can discipline yourself to be quick, to take the offensive, to dodge the enemies: fear, passivity, inertia, apathy.

It is important that you understand discipline in relationship to parent and child.

About a hundred years ago in Vienna many pregnant women died in the General Hospital after giving birth to their children. A Professor Klein said it was because of pollution from the atmosphere; a young doctor by the name of Philipp Semmelweis didn't believe it. Finally he discovered that childbed fever was blood poisoning brought about by contamination from the hands of medical students who examined the mothers. Professor Klein represented authority, the established order of things; Semmelweis represented freedom of thought, truth. Authority kicked Semmelweis out of the hospital, and for the rest of his days he fought for his principles, fought for the truth, but authority wouldn't listen. Finally Semmelweis examined a tissue specimen of a mother dead from childbed fever and cut his finger accidentally; he soon developed a fever and died—of childbed fever. In death he proved that freedom of thought could triumph over authority—even in tragedy.

There always will be a battle between authority and freedom of thought and its variation in the household, parental authority versus the freedom of expression of children.

Children have hope and the future on their side; adults

maturity and wisdom on theirs. Parental authority is unwise when it involves punishment, obstinancy, lack of understanding; this type of discipline brings about a gulf between parents and children.

Discipline properly executed on a child who secretly craves guidance must be helpful—rather than destructive, as was Dr. Klein's punishment of Dr. Semmelweis. Discipline is more a test of the adult who uses it than of the child who receives it. Understanding and self-respect are the guiding keys to creative discipline which will reach a child's heart.

Creative discipline is a partnership between a parent and a child—a meeting between the self-image of an adult who has made mistakes and the self-image of a youngster who will make mistakes. The atmosphere is one of friendship.

Thus a parent's effective discipline starts with self-discipline.

It is democratic; there is no force.

Coming back to the adult, as an adult, who tries to plan days of creative activity:

He must discipline himself to set goals every day.

He must discipline himself to his goals, enslave himself so that he can feel free.

He must discipline himself to think freely; he must not accept authority unthinkingly.

He must discipline himself in the spirit of sweetness with which a good parent would discipline a child who was a friend of his.

This is basic to a creative day.

6. *Imagination*. We all have the capacity of imagination and we must use it constructively. Imagination used destructively produces discontent; imagination used constructively produces confidence. You use your imagination constructively by utilizing the feel of past successes in your present undertakings. You use your imagination destructively by fretting about past failures. You must turn your back on negative feelings *now*—during your creative day.

We must see life in focus—within us, behind us, in front of us. Within us we must overcome our faults and habitually rise to our creative powers. Behind us are blunders which we should refuse to brood about, successes that we should reactivate. In front of us is today, potentially a glorious day, which our imagination must shape before we test it in reality.

Great statesmen use their imaginations to project into the realm of the possible images and ideas which lesser men would not dare imagine.

France's De Gaulle is such a seer; he has envisioned, "imagined" into reality, projects of glory to his country. Even his enemies see this.

To live a creative day, you must let your imagination function for you.

In the words of Ralph Waldo Emerson, "Imagination is not the talent of some but is the health of every man."

7. V for *Victory*. What should we do with the letter V? Shall V stand for victory in life or voluntary exile from life? Shall V stand for vitality or vacillation? Shall V stand for your venture toward a goal or the vacancy of your self-image?

During your creative day you must make the letter V stand for "V for Victory." Every day you must, like the little boy whose fingers I separated, make the "V for Victory" sign—in your mind.

If you fail today, after doing your best, then take aim on your goals tomorrow. Till you win.

You train yourself for victory every day as you train yourself to brush your teeth, eat your breakfast, put on your shoes.

You are victorious every day when you learn to free your creative machinery:

A. By worrying before you start for your goal, not after. If there are a number of roads toward your goal, anxiety is creative as you decide which road to take, but once you have selected your road, you stick to it without worry.

B. By responding to the present day, not yesterday.

C. By doing one thing at a time. Think of the hourglass. Which shall it be, one grain of frustration after another during your day or one grain of confidence after another? You make the decision.

D. By sleeping *on* a problem when it defies solution, not

sleeping *with* it. Your automatic servo-mechanism will work creatively for you, if you will let it.

E. By relaxing while you work. Confidence means relaxation, frustration means tension.

All of this means you are practicing the art of psycho-cybernetics, that is, steering your mind toward a creative productive goal.

You feel movement toward your goal, your creative day means movement. You encourage this movement.

Bill Bradley encouraged his success mechanism, as a youngster, by practicing and practicing his basketball skills —even after the other fellows left the court for the day.

Pete Gogolak, professional football's soccer-style place-kicker, practices his kicking over and over and over during the off-season. Sometimes it's lonely, but it pays off.

You, too, must keep driving if you want to win. Movement every day, a sense of direction toward a goal every day, no matter how small that goal may be. You keep moving in the stream of things, doing the best you can. And if you have no goal, you keep moving anyway—and a goal will catch up with you. Your sense of direction is forward.

8. *Eagerness*. In a creative day, you never withdraw from life; you feel an eagerness to be part of it. One daily goal is the eagerness to turn your back on negative feelings of the past, to accept and discard your failures.

Eagerness means desire. Desire is the heartbeat of your creative day; it is the promise of fulfilling your goal. With eagerness, you're *somebody;* without it, you're *nobody*.

A Frank Sinatra bounces back from his mistakes, with eagerness, and finds new areas in which to channel his talents and direct his success instincts.

But many people today believe that their years are full of defeat, uselessness, and preparation for death; there is no sparkle in their eyes. No eagerness at all.

You must feel the eagerness any human being feels when he likes himself and lives for the day.

You must concentrate on strengthening your image of yourself until you feel within you a sense of instant confidence, until you carry with you, eagerly, a functioning success mechanism in your daily pursuit of self-fulfillment.

Eagerness arouses the initiation of action; it is the launching pad of effort. And when you try, you are there; your create the power to reach your destination.

Your creative day consists in *trying* to be creative that day. Success means *trying* to succeed, *trying* to reactivate the success mechanism within you, *trying* to use your confidence. Failure means *trying* to fail, *trying* to reactivate the failure mechanism, *trying* to live in frustration.

What are you eager for? A creative day or a destructive day? You must make the decision.

9. *Daily growth.* You must keep inching forward. We all love to win, but often we are traitors to our success instincts. We must grow every day, train ourselves for triumph.

Success is within your grasp; your years can be meaningful. You must aim at growth, every day—if you stop coddling yourself, forgive the wounds which others have inflicted on you, and those which you have inflicted on them.

Time is precious. Make use of your creative day. We are here on earth for a very short time; we must not waste it.

It is never too late to tap your hidden resources. You must discover yourself and ascertain your true worth; you must stop shortchanging yourself. You must make this a daily task that makes you young and happy; every day is a challenge for you as an archaeologist digging under the debris of hurt feelings and resentments—your negative traits—to find the greatest treasure of all—your self-respect, your true self-image.

But we cannot live by ourselves. We must try to tap the hidden resources of others, too, to find their dignity. We must think twice before we judge others; we must look beyond their faces to the best of the real person.

Ralph Waldo Emerson once wrote: "And what is a weed? A plant whose virtues have not been discovered."

When did this thought occur to Emerson? Perhaps one day at harvest time, with the fields rippling in the wind, wheat for winter's bread. For, in those days, wheat was considered a useless weed.

Perhaps that day, gazing at the ripe bronze fields, Emerson was returning from a visit to his friend, the teacher Bronson Alcott. Perhaps he paused to weigh Alcott's idea that in school it was not the "bad boy" or the dullard who was to blame but those who lacked the patience to probe beneath the surface for good, however unpromising the surface. There were no "weeds" in Bronson Alcott's schoolroom.

No one is hopeless.

Again and again in clinic and hospital ward, I have seen the apparently hopeless misfit transformed into a useful person—a giver, not a taker—by a simple display of interest and belief in him. It always makes me wonder how many good citizens, creators and builders have been lost to us because someone somewhere, misled by the husk, did not see the golden grain within.

Each day we must strain for growth. We must not be useless "weeds" in life; we must grow to our full stature as sturdy oaks.

We must work to strengthen our positive image of ourselves so that we can project outward into success in life.

10. *Adjustment.* To live a creative day, you must adjust to the tensions of the day. Every day you must be ready for the problems that may beset you. You must develop the capacity to stand up under stress before you can firmly taste the rewarding moments in your day.

Adjustment implies faith—in others and in yourself.

Instead of negative feelings, we develop our nucleus of faith. Every cell has a nucleus of faith, a will to live. All those trillions of cells which make up a human being must fill with this will, this faith, this determination—to live.

We must have faith in ourselves. We must have imagination to illuminate our lives with the torch of the success mechanism. We remember that hope and faith are imagination on the wing soaring to a goal; frustration and despair are negative imagination with wings clipped.

It is easy to say "it can't be done."

Do you say it?

Do you say to yourself that—

there is no such thing as creative living?

to live is to be miserable?

people must somehow tolerate their years of suffering?

life is nothing but debts and taxes, aches and pains, with death around the corner?

If you do, you must revamp your thinking and develop a nucleus of faith to help you adjust to life.

Life is progressive, not retrogressive; it goes forward, not backward. We must forget regrets. We must rise above them or they will smother us.

We must believe in ourselves—like a Harry Truman who would not accept a defeat everyone predicted and woke up in the morning elected President of the United States; like a John Lindsay who scorned the underdog role and battled his way through to victory as Mayor of New York; like a Winston Churchill who felt no fear in the face of a German Nazi avalanche which had crushed men of less self-confidence.

To adjust to life, you must believe in yourself.

You may not be a Truman, a Lindsay, a Churchill—but they, too, are very human. All famous people are all-too-human. They, too, must fight to believe in themselves. They, too, must resolve their problems as sons, as brothers, as parents, as lovers; they, too, must struggle in their minds to find themselves.

Self-reproach is a pit of torture. The penalty for succumbing to it is heavy—both for the individual and for society. Your pacemaker, in creative living, must be your belief in yourself, which gives you expansive hope for your happiness.

When we doubt ourselves, we become difficult to get along with. We take out our feelings of inadequacy on our family, friends, acquaintances. We poison the atmosphere around us.

If you lack a nucleus of faith in yourself, you cannot enjoy your days. Faith in yourself, this can make you feel young.

We must work *every day* to strengthen our image of ourselves, rising above our failures to our successes.

Every day we must work to bolster our sense of worth—with compassion, with determination, with application.

"Impossible!" you say.

Then very day do the impossible.

Every day work in your mind to fortify yourself with the

faith in yourself that you need so that you can adjust yourself to life.

11. *Yearning for improvement.* This is the final component of your creative day. Yearning for improvement means renouncing the negative feelings that disfigure your self-image; it means focusing on positive life forces.

In your mind you move toward your productive energies. You love life and seek out its many challenges.

You turn your back on cynicism; you look for the good in life.

You rise above life's dangers, just as you have been able to resist the millions of bacteria in your nose and throat that would have destroyed you had you not possessed the life force to combat them.

You yearn to reach the qualities in yourself that you admire. You keep trying to make yourself a better person. You yearn for that sunny world within you as you walk away from your other world of darkness.

You make each day creative as you implement this yearning to reach the best that is in you.

Each day you reach into yourself for your best, and with it you move out into the world to live a happy day.

The Creative Person

These are the components of your creative day. I hope that you will find them helpful in planning the complexion of your life.

Summed up in one sentence, a person who lives creatively builds a feeling of strength in himself, accepts his failures compassionately, and projects his strength out into the world in the form of goals toward which he directs his energies.

He does not coddle himself with vast amounts of leisure time, which end up by boring him.

He does not place his faith in material goods; expensive automobiles or clothes or houses may be nice, but they are not basic.

He refuses to find magic in the names of geographical localities with pleasant climates.

He does not deluge himself with staggering varieties of passive entertainments.

He places his faith in himself. Accepting himself, he feels no need to withdraw into a passive pattern. He lives each day with enjoyment and fills his hours with goals.

He does not pity himself; he is too busy living.

In short, he lives with the eager goal-mindedness that a young person should feel—but often does not.

Is this the kind of living you want for yourself?

If you do, now is the time to start planning it, building the healthy self-image which is the basis of creative living.

Now is the time to start. You can't start too soon.

The Woman Who Wouldn't Give Up

Now let me tell you the story of my most difficult operation. It's the story of a woman with a beautiful self-image, a tiny woman who lived through horror and survived with a self-image ten feet tall.

I shall call her Anna. She was a very young Jewish woman living in Poland in 1942 during the Nazi occupation. The Nazis were liquidating the Warsaw ghetto. One day a German soldier tore her three-month-old child from Anna and threw it into the street like a cat. The baby was trampled to death. Anna then was thrown into a concentration camp, her husband into another. They thought each other dead. She was heartbroken, but refused to let her spirit be crushed.

Anna refused to admit defeat.

She worked as a slave laborer in an electric plant in Riga. One day the Germans shaved the women's hair off their heads. "The hair weighed me down," she said to a guard. "Now I can keep my head high. I have dignity, self-respect. No one can destroy that!"

The guard lifted his huge fist and bloodied her face, but Anna kept her head high.

One day she looked through the concentration camp gates and saw the fashionable townspeople taking a Sunday stroll. She saw children; one little girl had a flower in her hand. Anna thought, "Will I ever hold a flower in my hand again?"

She wept in silence in her dismal cell, but her head was high.

She had a glorious self-image in a rathole of despair. Someday, she vowed, she would hold a flower in her hand.

Three years later the Nazis were defeated. She was free! Hundreds of miles away her husband was freed. They found each other. In 1946 they came to America. Her son was born. He is now about twenty, studying to be a doctor.

"I want my son to recognize me," she said to me in my office recently. "Can you fix my face?"

It was a simple procedure, yet it was my most difficult operation. Usually a plastic surgeon operates on a facial scar to remove an inner scar. Here I was operating on Anna with the most beautiful young self-image I knew of. How could I give her a beautiful young face equal to it? At least I could try to bring her scarred face back to normal, a face whose chin was always up, to keep up with her strong self-image. The operation was successful—but the beauty of her face could never match the beauty of her self-image.

The last day I saw her she came holding a flower, a carnation, in her hand. She gave it to me. I put the carnation in my lapel proudly.

She wept then for the injustice of man. I wept inwardly for something far more important. I wept for her, though she didn't need it, for the dignity of man, for the flowing beauty of her self-image, for her self-respect as a person in God's' Image, refusing to be buried under the heavy weight of frustration at any time, anywhere!

Exercise 14

The courageous Anna vowed that someday, under better circumstances, she would once again hold a flower in her hand.

Now how about you when you have achieved something? Will you give yourself something, some acknowledgment of your success?

When you have fought through to a valued goal, when you have fortified your sense of self, will you give yourself a treat?

You have almost finished this book; you are working on the exercises; you feel better about yourself.

Well, now, how about a little reward?

Why not?

Go down the street to your florist, buy a flower, put a note in the box. Later the messenger brings the flower box to your apartment. You open the box, take out the note, and read it: "From an admirer!"

You take the flower from the box, go to the mirror, put it in your lapel if you're a man or in your hair if you're a woman, and say as you look in the mirror: "I have discarded the image of failure and frustration and have substituted the image of confidence and success. Sometimes I falter, but I keep trying. I deserve this flower!"

Still, your gift to yourself need not be a flower, which meant so much to Anna. Perhaps you'd rather buy a box of candy or a good cigar or a phonograph album—I can't tell you what.

Give yourself recognition. Give yourself credit for your hard-earned growth—not narcissistically—just in terms of the struggling man or woman you see in the mirror who tries so hard, each day, to set his goals and lead a creative day.

• 16 •

Your First Hour:

Launching a Creative Day

How do I sum up this book on creative living?

Perhaps I would do best to examine the nature of the life process and go on from there.

We are creatures of complexity; we are blood and tissue and water and bone; we are feelings and aspirations and intellectual abstractions; we live with grass and trees and mountains and animals.

Further, as twentieth-century people, we live with highways and automobiles and skyscrapers and airplanes and satellites and nuclear bombs.

So much complexity—within each area, so much complexity! Feelings so divergent, so varied; highways branching off in so many different directions.

You plan your years; how do you grapple with all this complexity?

Essentially, you do it by simplifying, by cutting away the red tape.

You see yourself as you are, one person among millions.

You see the main problems, and you deal with them one by one.

You see the uncertainties of your life, but you resolve to deal with them directly and courageously, not by frightened retreat.

You see the deadly pattern of passive living; you reject it..

You see, more and more clearly, that you must base the happiness of your years on—yourself. On your picture of yourself. On the strength of your self-image and the reactivation of your success mechanism.

Goals for the Creative

In writing this book, I have basically drawn from my own experience, my observations of friends and patients, and whatever wisdom my years of living have given me.

I have come to feel very strongly that you must see the necessity of setting goals to give you fire. You must go out into the world, capable of giving, taking, producing, doing.

In *The Art of Loving* (Harper & Bros., New York, 1956) psychologist Erich Fromm writes: "For the productive character, giving has an entirely different meaning. Giving is the highest expression of potency. In the very act of giving, I experience my strength, my wealth, my power. This experience of heightened vitality and potency fills me with joy. I experience myself as overflowing, spending, alive, hence as joyous. Giving is more joyous than receiving, not because it is a deprivation, but because in the act of giving lies the expression of my aliveness."

This is in harmony with the message of my book: the joy of producing.

Why should any rational person take away from himself this joy in doing, in living, in producing, just because some negative people may say to him, "You'd better watch yourself! Don't take any chances!"

This is like telling a kid of nine that he'd better not ride his bike or he'll fall off and hurt himself; or like telling an adolescent of sixteen that he'd better not play football or he'll end up in the hospital.

It is overprotection in the most negative sense. It is withdrawal from life; it is losing out in the war against negative feelings.

I reject this kind of talk; you should, too. Live the kind of life you can enjoy and be proud of—while you are blessed with the gift of life.

Your Finest Hour

In Chapter 15 we discussed the components of a creative day. But, to be even more specific, ready for action, let's discuss the most important hour of this creative day: your first hour.

This first hour is your springboard to send you spinning into a creative day.

And your first hour is yours. Your boss can't make demands on you, outsiders can't intrude. Here is your chance to get off to a good start.

Your first hour belongs to you; it is up to you to make it your finest hour. You must make each minute count.

Time is a relative concept. In each day there are twenty-four hours or 1440 minutes. But it is so easy to drift and waste your time; when you do, your time means nothing to you.

But, when you use it well, when you use it to set goals for the day that lies ahead, your first *hour* has 1440 minutes because your hour will make your day, because it will be your finest hour.

When you open your eyes and sit up in bed, stretch and look around your room, give yourself some good advice. Tell yourself that you will make this the best day you can. Tell yourself that today you will try to be human toward yourself, that you will forget yesterday's mistakes and live today. Tell yourself you have a right to make mistakes; do you know anyone who is perfect? Explain to yourself that you cannot be a success with others until you become a success with yourself. Understand that success is not an absolute; success is a process of rising above failure.

In the shower continue to give yourself a good pep talk. While the water pours down on you, refreshing your body, give some refreshment to your soul. See in your mind some of your good moments in life. Let the soap and water wash away the dirt as you wash away your negative feelings, realistically picturing the side of yourself that you like. See, see, see in your mind these pleasant images of yourself. Remind yourself that you were born to succeed, not to fail.

When you brush your teeth, look into the mirror and reinforce your sense of self. Don't be egotistical about it; you're not the only person around and don't pretend you are. But appreciate your image, with its imperfections, and appreciate the good in this face of yours, the human being behind the face. Siphon off the worries that assail you and come to grips with the reality of your image, of your being.

Your first hour must be your finest hour; you must gather momentum for a strong push into a good day.

You will have time to think while you are dressing. Don't waste your thoughts! Don't let them drift around aimlessly or speed up in a whirlpool of panic! Tell yourself, instead, that you have the right to be happy. Tell yourself that you have the right to achieve successes. Tell yourself that you must stop shortchanging yourself. Remind yourself that you are a unique human being, fashioned in God's Image, that you are *somebody*.

Your first hour is a critical hour; it is an hour of decision. You are deciding whether you will go all-out to launch a day of creative living or whether you will defeat yourself and crawl into a cave to hide. Possibly, external events will block the achievement of your goals today, that is true. But even if they do, you will have fought the good fight and will feel satisfaction from this knowledge. And then, there is always tomorrow.

Once more, during this precious first hour, return to the mirror—to shave or apply your lipstick or perhaps to comb your hair or wash your face. Once more, look at yourself; this is the only self you've got. You must develop a healthy liking for yourself; if you don't, you're through.

As you finish your physical preparations for the day, plan your goals. What is it you want to accomplish today? And what tactics will you use? List your goals in your mind but, first, make sure that these goals enthuse *you*. If others think your goals are silly, this is unimportant if they have real meaning for you. You build enthusiasm for real living today during this first hour when you plan your goals.

Your vital first hour ends when you nourish your body with breakfast, firing it with energy to go out into the world geared for creative living.

The Man Who Grew More Creative

Productive living is a reality—even for people living with demands and tension. Let me tell you another story.

Every year graduates of my class from the College of Physicians and Surgeons at Columbia University held their annual dinner. I had meant to attend, I had wanted to go often, but somehow some last-minute crisis would always force itself upon me. Through these twists of fate, I had never attended one of these dinners.

Then the annual invitation came—it was the thirtieth anniversary of our graduation. I resolved that nothing would keep me from this dinner.

Old Charlie would be there, Charlie, the coatroom attendant. I thought affectionately of the interest he had taken in me when I was a young student—the interest he had taken in all of us.

Carefully I dressed for the class reunion, and I arrived on time. I roamed around the cocktail lounge outside the dining hall; it was full of people and I looked for some of the old familiar faces I hadn't seen for thirty years. I didn't recognize anyone at all.

Finally I saw one: I knew that fellow. Damn! I had been looking into a mirror; it was only me.

As the evening wore on, I relocated my old college chums. It was no easy task. How they had changed! How they had aged! Where had the youth gone; where was the sparkle in their eyes? So many of them looked tired.

I felt shocked when they exclaimed, on seeing me, "How you've changed, Max!"

There was a raised platform at the end of the huge dining room: the guests of honor sat on the platform. I recognized one immediately; it was Charlie the coatroom attendant.

I marveled at his youthful appearance, more than ever when an old friend told me that Charlie was eighty-six. We talked about the secret of his remaining youthful; my friend felt it was because he helped everyone, had a kind word for everyone, adopted the struggling young doctors-to-be as almost children of his, and gave us support when we needed it.

I felt sure that this was the secret of his youth. But how about Boysie?

I remembered Professor James Boysland well for his extraordinary skill as a surgeon. There he sat, at the table of the class of 1903; it was the fiftieth anniversary of their graduation. The survivors of this class looked very old; their eyes lacked luster and their backs were bent. But Boysie sat erect in his chair, his eyes alert and clear. His carriage, his manner reminded me of a young man.

After dinner I went over to talk to him. I told him how well he looked and asked him for his secret.

Professor Boysland offered me a cigar and took a sip of brandy. He said he was something of a Dr. Jekyll and Mr. Hyde, a man living two lives at the same time.

Taking a small object from his pocket, he placed it on the table in front of me. It was a figurine of a dancing girl, carved from wood.

"Do you like it?"

On tiptoe, arms flung out, head tossed back, it was a glorious symbol of freedom. I nodded yes.

"I'll tell you about the sculptor."

Boysie talked about the war years, the shortage of doctors,

the operations he was performing day and night—until his tension brought on sleepless nights.

One evening, leaving the hospital after operating, he heard the wail of a newborn baby. He found himself thinking about the baby: was it a boy or a girl? What did it look like? What adventures lay in the future?

Arbitrarily, Boysie decided it was a boy, plotted out his physical appearance, arranged the outline of his life. The baby would grow up to be a doctor: at the age of twelve, he would realize what his vocation was to be.

A realization dawned on him. The imaginary baby—twelve years old then in his mind—was himself.

"Then I began to envy this twelve-year-old me. I wished that I could change places with him, begin over again. What would I do next? I would start reading medical books to prepare for my career."

Then Boysie found his rising excitement blocked. He saw himself as this eager, growing twelve-year-old boy pouring over medical books, but what next? When he read the books, he would not be able to feel eager; he was too familiar with them already.

Then, he thought, why did the twelve-year-old Boysie have to be a doctor? Why not another field? For days he argued with himself, looking for another field in which to channel the energies of the ardent twelve-year-old Boysie.

"Then I saw. Young Boysie had artistic talent, and he liked to sketch. And . . ."

Professor Boysland pointed to the figure.

". . . he became a sculptor."

Fascinated, I thought about what Boysie had said. His method was perhaps indirect, but the results were spectacular. He had two lives now, two fields in which to function, in which to direct his productive energies.

The extra work didn't tire him; it relaxed him. When the "Old Boysie" came home after a hard day's work as a surgeon, the "Young Boysie" would work as sculptor and cheer him. Young and old seemed to shake hands, bridging the years, bringing youth. There were no more sleepless nights.

Back at my table, I smiled as I thought of the twelve-year-old boy seeing the world from the old man's placid eyes.

Boysie's concept of creativity had great impact on me as I grew older. A plastic surgeon all my life, I have turned more and more to writing and lecturing in my later years.

As with Boysie, this extra work does not tire me; I feel an increased sense of boyish excitement when I write and when I lecture. I feel younger.

I feel that all people can learn a valuable lesson from this old-young man.

Your Untapped Wealth

It is a tragedy that, throughout history, so few people have fully exploited their potentialities. For almost all people have rich, untapped areas of talent.

Don't be a "doubting Thomas." Follow the example of the "Thomas" I've written about, Thomas Edison.

Or of another "Thomas," Thomas Jefferson, America's third President.

Thomas Jefferson's accomplishments, also, are almost beyond belief. His confidence in his powers must have been extraordinary.

In the process of serving out two full terms in our nation's highest office, he negotiated the famed Louisiana Purchase, which some historians have called the outstanding bargain in American history.

This was preceded, of course, by his famed drafting of our great Declaration of Independence.

Jefferson's other achievements as a statesman are too numerous to mention. Few American statesmen in our history have done so much; it is doubtful if any have done more.

But the astonishing thing about Jefferson was his full use of his creative powers in other fields as well. A married man with two daughters, he was president of the American Philosophical Society, established the University of Virginia, supported the first American scientific expeditions. He was also a top-flight architect, who designed not only his own home, but those of friends.

I am not suggesting that you are in any way a failure if

you cannot measure up to such monumental achievements as those of Thomas Jefferson.

My message is simply that you should reach out to the world with your full capabilities, whatever they may be, that you should emulate him in utilizing your resources, instead of blocking them.

No Blackout for Your Goals

While writing this book, I was one of millions inconvenienced by the power failure which crippled a huge area on the eastern coast of the United States. My lights were out; my phone was dead.

I lit a candle and located my transistor radio, learning that nine states were hit, thirty million people in darkness.

The blackout fell at about 5:30 P.M. I had to catch the 9 A.M. plane for California the following morning; I was scheduled to lecture.

The lightless night passed, hour upon dark hour. I went to bed early, but could not sleep. I argued with myself.

"Why worry? No one can blame you for not going. Go next week."

"No, I was looking forward to lecturing, and I'm going."

It was like a tennis match. I batted the ball back and forth.

At 3:30 A.M. the lights were still out, the elevator was dead. Living on the eighteenth floor was no advantage in this situation.

Finally I decided that I was going toward my goal. I grabbed hat, coat, two grips, candle—and opened the door to the stairway. In candlelight I dimly saw stairs and stairs and more stairs below me.

Then I dropped the candle and saw nothing at all.

What to do? In a wave of negativism, I told myself to retire back to my home and give up on what I wanted to do. But I overcame these negative thoughts and proceeded toward my goal.

Step by step I inched my way down to the seventeenth floor, walking slowly, carefully, down to the sixteenth, the fifteenth, the fourteenth ... When I stood on New York's still-dark sidewalks I dropped the luggage with a thud; I felt as if I had just released a couple of five hundred pound weights.

I was halfway toward my goal, only; I still had to get a taxi to take me to the airport. I stumbled around, waving my hands. Getting a taxi seemed impossible.

I figured a cab would need an hour to get to the airport. At 7:55 a taxi stopped for me—just in time. Departure time for the plane was 9 A.M.

I turned my back to claim my luggage, picked it up. The taxi was moving off without me.

After my first reaction of anger, I felt despair. "I did my best," I told myself. "I'll go back to sleep."

"No," my more positive side urged, "you can still make it."

And I did. A responsible cabdriver stopped shortly, took a few seasoned shortcuts, drove me swiftly, safely, and I made the plane. Hours later I was in San Francisco, then Monterey. I enjoyed speaking, enjoyed my trip—more so because *I* had not blacked out.

I felt good because in the battle in my mind of my success and failure instincts, my success instincts had won out, and I had not let adverse circumstances keep me from my goal.

My story is illustrative, not an exercise in self-congratulation. Truthfully, I have failed myself many, many times in my life, and some of my failures I have described in this book. Still, even as I grow older, entering into the sixties and on past sixty-five, I feel happy that I am not falling into the nonliving blackout which crushes so many people. In harnessing my active, goal-oriented success instincts, I strengthen my enjoyment of life all the time.

The power-failure blackout affected thirty million people for a short time; emotional blackout crushes millions more every day—and for all their lives.

You must resist the emotional blackout of negative feelings that would keep you from living creatively. You can pull out of it if you understand the areas of darkness.

Exercise 15

There are fifteen exercises in this book which I feel will help you on the road to creative living. This is the last one, and I'm going to make the last the first. About the first hour, that is.

Because it is your first hour of each day that you have the opportunity to set the tone for your day. It is in this first hour that you must guard against emotional blackout and bring forward all your inner positive forces to thrust forward into a world which is coming to life from sleep once again.

In this first hour you must spring forward toward a creative day—with concentration, affirmation, and eagerness.

In this first shaping hour, you must launch yourself into a creative day. The day is basic. For, if you add day to day, you are living creative weeks, months, years—and you have mastered the art of creative living today.

You must act *now*, not tomorrow. Delay is deadly. And, when you get into the habit of making full use of your first hour, you are on your way to a *now, let's go, no-nonsense* way of thinking that can only help you to channel your life in positive directions.

This, then, is my advice to help you avoid the emotional blackout which is one of the unfortunate symptoms of our times: *launch yourself for creative living during your first hour*.

Imagine that you are sitting in a comfortable chair; the only light on in the room is by your chair.

Then imagine that you turn the light off, plunging the room into total darkness. You can see nothing; the blackout makes you feel helpless.

Now imagine that you turn the light on. You can see once again. You have won out over your little blackout.

In your imagination, then, you are seeing the great difference between emotional blackout—helplessness—and emotional enlightenment—vision.

If you prefer to do this exercise more directly, turn out the light in your room, sit in the dark awhile, then turn on the light.

As your final exercise, enlighten yourself: turn on the light in your mind. Give yourself some last advice to guard against emotional blackout:

1. Understand that you must make your minutes count during your first hour each day. You must use them to strengthen your self-image, to plan your goals, to get ready for a good day ahead.

2. In the important minutes of your first hour, you must also regroup to weed out the negative feelings which would obstruct your day. You must escalate your war against negative feelings so that you can enjoy life.

3. During this first hour, you must reaffirm your right to the good things in life, to the good feelings in life, to the good thoughts in life.

Every day, when you wake up, tell yourself that this is your first hour, this is your key hour, and this must be your finest hour so you can start a good day.

Reread this chapter again and again so that you will remind yourself that creative living starts during your first hour, when you come back from sleep into the world.

Many Happy Years for You

It is my hope that you will use well the minutes of your first hour every day, leading into creative days, which will add up to many happy years.

You don't have to envy the achievements of others—not if you develop your own individual creativity.

I wish you years of creative living that will enable you to rise to your true stature.

It is your responsibility to yourselves to fill the picture in, to give yourselves the right to create a happy life.

It is no downhill, one-way street; nothing in life that is worthwhile is easy.

But, if you make it your daily task to make peace with yourself, to accept yourself, to plunge toward life *with* yourself, you may realistically have great hopes for happy days and years in this world—today.

Index